OVERLORDS OF ATLANTIS
AND THE
GREAT PYRAMID

INNER LIGHT PUBLICATIONS

EDITORIAL DIRECTION
& LAYOUT:
TIMOTHY GREEN BECKLEY

For information: Inner Light Publications
Box 753, New Brunswick, N.J. 08903.

Cover Art by Vicki Khuzami

Typesetting by Soltec Manuscript Service

ISBN: 0-938294-63-6

CONTENTS

In the great days of ancient Egypt it is believed that giant crystals were placed at the top of the pyramids and were utilized as energy devices and as beacons for star travelers. (Art by Carol Ann Rodriguez)

I

Atlantis: A World Before Our Own

Traditionally, Atlantis was a continent in the Atlantic Ocean. Shaken by a series of violent cataclysms, it sank below the surface of the waters —where, logically, glaciers and weather could not get at it.

Mankind appears to have regretted this loss; some years ago a public opinion poll found that the people in the United States would rank the discovery of Atlantis as great a news story as the Second Coming of Christ.

I have come to believe the civilization on Earth has been cyclical and that there have been highly evolved human or hominid cultures before our present epoch. Atlantis may be but a symbol of man's racial memory of that time before our own. Within man's collective unconscious may lie half-forgotten memories of a time when man-creatures lived in god-like splendor while *Homo sapiens* groveled in awe of his magnificent predecessors. This book will be a search to define that time and those dimly remembered god-men.

If Atlantis existed, where was its geographical location? Surely not in the Atlantic Ocean, as is commonly supposed, declared the research of Dr. W. Maurice Ewing, oceanography and professor of geology at Columbia University, who, in a 1953 expedition aboard the *Devin Moran*, issued the pronouncement that the floor of the Atlantic had never been above water.

Dr. Ewing used the oil exploration techniques of seismographic recordings to identify the rock under sea-floor sediment. "We found that the rocks under every part of the ocean are completely different from those under the continents," he states. "This discovery tends to support the theory that the continents are distinct entities and that the ocean floor was never above water."

While proponents of the Atlantis-beneath-the-Ocean school huddled together in their scattered small groups and commiserated about their alienation from modern science, they found, in 1956, an unexpected ally from the hallowed halls of orthodoxy. Dr. Rene Malaise of the Riks Museum in Stockholm, Sweden, offered new evidence that a land such as Atlantis might very well have existed in the Atlantic. According to Dr. Malaise, his colleague, Dr. P. W. Kolbe, had furnished proof of the sinking of a Mid-Atlantic Ridge.

Dr. Kolbe found this proof in the tiny shells of diatoms, minuscule marine animals, when he took a core sample at a depth of 12,000 feet in the tropical Atlantic. According to Dr. Kolbe's examination of the shells, some of the diatoms were exclusively the fresh-water type. "They could only have been deposited in the sediment when it was part of a fresh-water lake," Dr. Malaise said in making his announcement of his colleague's findings. "The only way that they could have been deposited in a fresh-water lake would be for the present sea bottom to have been above sea level at one time."

In the opinion of Dr. Malaise, there was once a Mid-Atlantic Ridge that settled beneath the surface of the ocean as recently as 10,000 to 12,000 years ago.

"The ridge stood as a barrier to the Gulf Stream, landlocking the Arctic Ocean from Europe to Greenland," the Swedish scientist pointed out. "When the land barrier sank, the Gulf Stream reached the Arctic Ocean and the Ice Age ended. The whole history of the world was affected by the climatic change brought about by the sinking of Atlantis."

In 1963, Professor Georgly Lindberg of the Soviet Union's Zoological Institute of the Academy of Sciences was quoted in a *Tass* news release: "The hypothesis that there is a North Atlantic continent, presently submerged 4,500 to 5,000 meters of water, is confirmed by new findings." However, Soviet scientists said that the submerged continent could hardly have been the highly advanced civilization referred to by the ancient writers, such as Plato and Plimy, for, in their estimation, the continent mentioned by Professor Lindberg sank some time before the end of the Tertiary geological period, which began around 60 million years ago and ended a million years ago.

No, the continent could not have been Atlantis. Not unless one is willing to grant man, or some form of hominid life, a much earlier cultural history than scientists have thus far been able to concede.

Rolling Back the History of Civilization

However, if archaeologists continue to roll back the history of civilization in such leaps and bounds as they have been in recent years, it seems unavoidable that they will find that they have pushed themselves into a series of civilizations that preceded the cultural epoch of which we are a part. If the archaeologists are able to approach their findings free of professional demands requiring them to fit every stone and artifact into a ready-made and academically approved slot, it seems likely that they will thereby confirm the theories that many responsible scholars have long held concerning the possibility of other cultural life cycles on this planet— each destroyed, perhaps, by some great natural or man-precipitated catastrophe.

Less than four decades ago, for example, it was generally believed that if man did exist in America even 5,000 years ago, he was nothing more than a primitive hunter. Then, in 1952, Dr. Paul Sears of Yale University dug up some maize pollen grains from about 240 feet below the surface of the dried lake bed on which Mexico City is built.

Maize is the most highly developed agricultural plant in the world, so highly developed that scientists have never been able to trace its original ancestors. According to radiocarbon testing, the pollen grains from the Mexican lake bed are at least 25,000 years old.

Someone was harvesting domesticated maize in the Americas at least 20,000 years before anyone was supposed even to be smashing slow animals with rock clubs. Dr. Sears commented that anthropologists would now have to hunt the ancestors of Mexican Man, as well as those of corn, much earlier than they had thought necessary.

Reports of a dawn man 15 to 20 millions of years old found in an Italian coal mine were released in the mid-1950s. Dr. Helmutt de Terra of Columbia University told journalists in Rome that a section of jawbone, along with the bones of the feet and hands of *Oreopithecus*, had been found.

Java and Peking men go back a mere 300,000 years, a few ticks of the cosmic clock compared to 15 to 20 million. If anthropoids such *Oreopithecus* were flourishing at the very dawn of time, why could not a more sophisticated species of *Homo sapiens* have co-existed with them, just as twentieth-century Australians once coexisted with stone age aborigines?

And if not *Homo sapiens*, perhaps an alien form of hominid life brought to Earth by spaceships from another world.

In 1968, geologists worked themselves into a lather over a fossilized sandal print unearthed near Delta, Utah. A fossilized sandal print is exciting enough, but William Meister found a rock with two tiny trilobites embedded in the print. Trilobites, as any textbook will pronounce, date back to the earliest geologic breakdown of the Paleozoic era, roughly 500 million years ago.

Dr. H. Doelling of the Utah Geological Survey, in perhaps unintentional understatement, said that the whole business just did not fit together with geological history. Trilobites simply were not contemporaneous with human beings. At least not according to the standard, academically approved geological-anthropological scale.

As more of these scientific anomalies are unearthed and we learn more about prehistory, the persistent "catastrophic theory of history"should gain more credence among reputable scientists.

Humanity's Fall and the Great Flood

As we have already noted, the catastrophic theory of history maintains that there have been a number of highly cultured and technological civilizations in pre-history that were almost completely destroyed by a disaster of some kind. Coupled with the notion of great, vanished, prehistoric cultures is the universal legend that, at one time, gods walked upon the earth in direct intercourse with man until a dramatic "fall" separated man from direct communication with the deities.

Closely linked with the myth of an earthly paradise from which man was expelled, or from which the gods withdrew, is the world-wide cultural memory of a great flood, or natural catastrophe, that destroyed all civilization as it then existed. Many Atlantean theorists see the universal flood story as being directly related to Atlantis's sinking beneath the sea.

Greek scientist A. G. Galanopoulos and American oceano-graphic engineer James E. Mavor believe that a small-scale "Atlantis" was blasted into folklore by a gigantic Karakatoa-type volcanic explosion. Immanuel Velikovsky (*Worlds in Collision*) maintains that the catastrophe was caused by the near-collision of the planet Venus with Earth. While a world-wide deluge might be rather hard to accept, the notion that survivors of the Atlantean disaster might have spread the tale of their great civilization's sudden destruction to primitive peoples on all continents becomes, it seems, a much more palatable pill to swallow.

Although we can no longer accept the clerical dictum that Earth was formed at 9:00 A.M., 4004 B..C. on October 23, the fact remains that the multi-cultural memory of a great flood influences an calendar of our present epoch. Since historical records are found only up to approximately 5000 B.C. it is generally agreed that our epoch has existed for something under 7,000 years. The evidence now seems to indicate, however, that if there were a Great Deluge of nearly global consequence, or even a localized catastrophe that snuffed out the acme of culture at that time, it probably occurred earlier than 5000 B.C.

In the January, 1969, issue of *Fate* magazine, Hugh Auchincloss Brown reports on the evidence that indicates that the Temple of Serapis at Pozzuoli on the Adriatic Sea's Gulf of Venice was erected by artisans of a civilization that existed 12,000 to 19,000 years ago. Brown writes that the temple must have been erected when the site was *above* sea level by at least some 20 feet, judging by the holes left by boring clams 15 to 20 feet above the present sea level.

The creators of the great marble columns had tools that enabled their workmanship to rival the Egyptians'. According to Brown: "The present location of Pozzuoli is approximately 46 degrees N. Latitude, but at the time the Temple was erected its latitude was 40 degrees. The earth did a roll-around which was caused by the eccentric rotating mass of ice at the North Pole, and Pozzuoli moved to approximately 65 degrees N. Latitude at which time the temple was submerged."

In 1966, an oceanographic research expedition led by Dr. Robert J. Menzies of Duke University aboard the vessel *Anton Brunn* photographed what appeared to be carved rock columns under 6,000 feet of ocean in the Milne-Edward Deep, a depression that reaches a depth of nearly 19,000 feet. A cautious Dr. Menzies admitted that the discovery of what *may be* the ruins of an ancient city could be "one of the most exciting discoveries of this century, insofar as ruins go."

Some of the columns are half-buried in mud, while others stand upright. Many of them appear to have a kind of writing on them. There are old Inca ruins on the nearby coast of Callao, the port of Lima, Peru, but a city resting beneath 6,000 feet of water would have to be many thousands of years older than the ancient coastal cities.

In 1955, William Mardorf, an ex-Marine skin diver, took photographs of submerged ruins at a depth of 95 feet in Bolivia's Lake Titicaca, the highest navigable lake in the world. Massive docks for ships have been cut out of solid stone in the titicaca area, leading some researchers to theorize that this high plateau was once a sea port until some dramatic geological change rearranged the topography.

Diving For Atlantis Off Bimini

When I first met John Alexander, he was an infantry captain based at Scofield Barracks, Honolulu. He was also the Silva Mind Control representative Hawaii, and well known as a lecturer on precataclysmic civilizations.

"For a long time there has been a premise that the military automatically stifles one's thinking," the boyishly handsome Captain Alexander smiled. "I must say that it has given me more time to do research. I have been around the world a couple of times. I have been in Special Forces — the Green Berets is my special field — and took advantage of my hitches in Vietnam to study Buddhism."

As a Green Beret Underwater Demolition expert, Captain Alexander rates as an extremely experienced diver. Since he had personally explored and photographed the Bimini site, I was delighted when our mutual friend, Dr. Patricia Diegel, brought us together for an interview.

When did you do your diving?

CAPTAIN ALEXANDER: June of 1971. When you are diving and all of a sudden you run into a series of megaliths, there is no doubt in your mind that you are seeing something very different from ocean floor. You can compare the size of some of these slabs when you see a diver next to them. Some weighed thousands of pounds, and they form very, very huge regular angles. Some run six to eight feet square in that particular site. Others are fifteen to forty feet long, and they look as through they have been inlaid into one another.

And yet you feel that you have seen but a small section of what must be a much larger city?

Oh, yes. I got down there and just swam as far as I could, and there were so many more things that I simply could not begin to see.

Dr. Mason Valentine says that this is one of a series of sites which we can trace all the way to the Yucatan and which also extend much farther north.

Are there any criticisms of the site put forth by the scientific community?

The most common is that the site is probably sea turtle pens. Sea turtles are quite a valuable commodity in the area, but we are talking about someone moving untold tons of rocks just to keep turtles from straying.

What is the composition of the stones?

Well, there are various types of stones in various sites. Dating and composition work have been done on some pillars, and I understand — "from a confidential and reliable source," I believe is the legal terminology — that the analysis came out as *pink marble*.

This particular kind of marble is mined in only three placed today — Italy, Sicily and Crete. I hardly need point out that the site of Bimini is thousands of miles away from any of these areas, which leaves to possibilities: 1.) There was a technology capable of bringing this material to the site; or 2.) there was another quarry in another land that was above water at the time. Another theory was that ships in the fifteenth century or so had been using pink marble as ballast. When the ships sank, the wood rotted and the marble ballast remained. Well, this structure is 1,800 meters long, so that sailing vessel would have had to have been the size of an aircraft carrier!

Would you state without equivocation that the structures off Bimini are the remnants of a precataclysmic civilization?

Oh, yes, these artifacts far predate the Aztec or the Mayan civilizations, as well. The area in which we found these artifacts has not been above water for at least 10,000 years.

A lot of people tend to think of Atlantis as a lost island or city under the ocean, but we believe that it was a fairly massive continent. A great deal of work has been done linking Atlantis to the Minoan culture. I don't think this association is entirely satisfactory, but it may be part of the answer. We feel that the Atlanteans were advanced enough to be an expanding civilization with outposts.

Some researchers believe the Canary Islands to be the topmost peaks of a submerged Atlantean mountain range.

These outposts would be affected by the great cataclysm, of course, but not to the degree that the main continent. We feel that some of the findings in Central Mexico and the Yucatan indicate that there was communication with Atlantis. There is so much universality of culture and cultural designs around the world that we feel the Atlantean influence was extremely far-reaching.

How advanced were they? Would you put their civilization about equal with our own?

I will go along with Edgar Cayce and some of the clairvoyants who say that the second civilization was the one that really reached an advanced state of technology. They certainly had the capability of heavier-than-air flight, subterranean areas with self-contained atmospheric conditions, and an energy source far beyond that which we have attained.

Submerged and Lost Cities

In 1954, German archaeologist Jurgen Spanuth believed that he had found Atlantis under the North Sea five miles north of Heligoland. After exploring the sunken, walled city that lay beneath 50 feet of water, Spanuth was convinced that he had truly found the remnants of an advanced civilization.

Using Plato as his guide, Spanuth read that two of the principal landmarks of Basilea, the capital of Atlantis, were the royal citadel and the great temple. As Plato repeats the legend, Basilea lay approximately six miles from the coast and was encircled by a 3,035-foot wall. Spanuth's underwater city yielded an almost undamaged wall with a circumference of 3,956 feet.

Spanuth did not feel that Plato's date of 8000 B.C. was accurate for the sinking of Atlantis, however. He estimated that the city in the North Sea had submerged around 1200 B.C., roughly 800 years before Plato's time.

There seems little doubt that Spanuth located a city of an advanced ancient civilization. The streets of the city were paved with molded slabs of firestone, and there was ample evidence to indicate that the forgotten inhabitants had mastered the craft of smelting ore.

The Great Palace of Knossus on Crete

Other scholars and field archaeologists have championed the great civilization of Crete as the logical pretender to the throne of Atlantis. Crete, destroyed in some as yet undetermined manner in 1400 B.C., had its great palace of Knossus situated three miles from the sea. The palace was one of the greatest wonders of the ancient world and typified the Minoan peoples' passion for art.

Reverend James Baikie, who assisted in the excavation of Knossus, once said that his impression of ancient Minoan artisans was that of ". . . a people of astonishing mental agility, extraordinarily alert and sensitive to original ideas, and sometimes overflowing in the very fullness of its life. . . . To turn from the reliefs of an Assyrian palace to the frescoes of Knossus is like turning from shambles to a green meadow in spring time."

The citizens of Knossus boasted fresh water piped into their homes, an efficient drainage system; and flush toilets in the palace. Dr. Angelo Mosso, an Italian archaeologist, told of observing the ancient sewer system one day after a heavy downpour of rain. "All the drains acted perfectly," he said, "and I saw the water flow from sewers through which a man could walk upright. I doubt if there is another instance of a drainage system acting after 4,000 years."

Dr. Mosso examined the terra cotta pipes that connected with the main drainpipe in the palace, the faucets, the system of latrines, a complete sanitary system that Europe did not regain for more than 3,000 years. The Italian archaeologist confessed that he looked with admiration on a certain latrine in the queen's room. "In a little room, lined with alabaster, was a wooden seat 57 centimeters in height from the pavement, while beneath the latrine passed one branch of the sewer. I saw another less handsomely appointed in the palace of Phaestos. To us hygienists, these are two remarkable points of excellence."

In the July, 1957, issue of *Fate* magazine, editor Curtis Fuller suggests that the clue to the mysterious disappearance of the Minoan culture has been with us for centuries and we have been misreading it: "For in the *Timaeus* Plato tells how Solon, when in Egypt, was told of an island in the Western sea which had been a great power holding sway over other islands and over parts of the continent," Fuller writes. "This fabled state was overwhelmed by the sea as a judgment of the gods. Plato went into great detail to describe the island, and (Rev. James) Baikie says that his details are such as to leave practically no doubt that Solon's Egyptian priest was actually describing what he had heard of the port and palace of Knossus."

Texts in a script called Minoan Linear B, deciphered about 1956 after years of study by Michael Ventris, a London architect, show that men named Achilles, Hector, and Orestes owned property on the island of Crete about 3,200 years ago. Is it mere coincidence that men who were probably the military lords of Knossus bear the names of Homeric heroes? Was Crete, inundated by the sea in a terrible natural catastrophe, the basis of the Atlantis legend? Did the ancient Greeks borrow more heavily from the Minoan culture than has yet been supposed? Or did both the Minoans and the Greeks seek to emulate an earlier and greater civilization that existed beyond the pillars of Hercules (Strait of Gibraltar)?

Ancient Tartessos

In the 1920s, Professor Adolf Schulten of Erlangen University, together with the archaeologist Bonsor and the geologist Jessen, unearthed what he thought, according to the Greek historian Strabo's direction, was the site of ancient Tartessos. Since that time, many scholars and theorists have concluded that the fabled Atlantis and the lost city of Tartessos are one and the same.

Tartessos, the Tarshish of the Old Testament, flourished from 1100 B.C. until its destruction in 500 B.C. Tartessos was the capital of a nation whose culture was rich and advanced, and it was probably the earliest city-state in the pre-Roman West. Although the city is described in the journals of several ancient geographers and historians, people have been searching for the site of Tartessos for over 2,000 years.

The lure of Atlantis has called author-researcher Brad Steiger to Polynesia, to Egypt, Israel, Jordan and to Native-American power places throughout the United States and Canada, seeking additional clues to the mysterious "lost world." Here he pauses before a wall of ancient Egypt.

The land is marshy where Tartessos once stood — probably at the mouth of the Guadalquivir River on the coast of Spain — and the once rich land is now buried beneath several layers of silt. As the legends told of Atlantis sinking into the sea and becoming inundated, so do the writers of antiquity record how the Guadalquivir's channels became reduced in number from three to one and subsequently covered the island city-state at its mouth.

Schulten's research has convinced many Atlantean scholars that a number of convincing parallels exist between the evidence unearthed at Tartessos and the account of the fabled Atlantis described in the works of Plato.

According to Plato's *Critias*, Atlantis stood on an island surrounded by three rings of water. Tartessos is known to have been an island city located between the three mouths of the Guadalquivir.

Plato provides a detailed account of the canal system of Atlantis. A writer of antiquity describes a similar system of canals being used in Tartessos.

Atlantis is said to have been the wealthiest nation that has ever existed. Tartessos is referred to in ancient records as "the wealthiest city in the world."

Plato seems to have been intrigued by the cult of the bull that flourished in Atlantis. The worship of the bull, with attendant graceful maneuvers executed between its horns, is also known to have a once-active cult in ancient Crete. "Bull vaulting" could have come to Tartessos from Crete and survived in Spain as the national sport of bull fighting.

Atlantis, according to the Greek philosopher's account, was the greatest maritime power the world had ever known. The ships of Tartessos are recorded to have spanned the entire Mediterranean, and are said to have reached Scotland, perhaps even Iceland and North America. The Old Testament speaks of the "ships of Tarshish" and gives scriptural substantiation to their far-reaching voyages.

Again it is Strabo who testifies that the culture of Tartessos was advanced and intellectually active. He records that the citizens of Tartessos had prose accounts, poems, and a legal system that even then were 6,000 years old.

The Island of Santorini

In the early 1960s, Dr. Angelos Galanopoulos, a seismologist and professor of geophysics at the University of Athens, believed that he discovered a 2,600-year-old error that an ancient Greek scholar had made when translating the legend of Atlantis from the works of Egyptian priests. The Egyptians used similar symbols for the numbers 10 and 100, and the ancient translator confused them and incorrectly wrote that Atlantis was ten times larger than it actually had been. If Atlantis was really only one-tenth the size traditionally ascribed to it, Dr. Galanopoulos reasoned, it could very easily have been an island in the Mediterranean, rather than a large continent in the Atlantic.

Dr. Jelle de Boer, a young geologist who was a research fellow at Wesleyan University, stated that his research tended to support the theory put forth by Dr. Galanopoulos. A group of geologists had determined that a volcanic eruption had occurred near the island of Crete, center of the culturally advanced Minoan civilization, about 1500 B.C. the island of Santorini, according to geologists, had erupted and disappeared in a violent volcanic catastrophe. The enormity of the blast had caused huge tidal waves, fires, and loss of oxygen in the air on Crete, which was known in Egypt as Atlantis.

Dr. Galanopoulos soon acquired James W. Mavor, Jr., of the Woods Hole Oceanographic Institution, as an ally. Mavor contributed the use of the research vessel *Chain*, and worked on and around Santorini (also called Thera) in 1965-66, until he became satisfied that the island had been a part of Atlantis. Mavor and other scientists theorized that Santorini had exploded with a blast the equal of 2,000 H-bombs, five times the force of that which destroyed the East Indian island of Krakatoa in 1883. Such a cataclysm perhaps the greatest ever experienced by man, would surely have been transformed into legend, the history of the time.

The principal point on which the Santorini-Atlantis theory hinges is that Plato, who was a philosopher, not a historian, claimed that he got the legend from a relative, who had heard it from his grandfather, who had heard it from his father, who heard it recounted by the Athenian leader Solon, who had first heard it from an Egyptian priest. Now no academic anthropologist or historian is going to accept for one minute Ignatius Donnelly's notion that the Egyptians had the legend in their tradition because Egypt had been the major Atlantean colony. The academicians will, rather, suggest that an oral tradition does not make the most reliable or convincing kind of evidence. And since Plato included the details of Atlantis in two dialogues, *Timeus* and *Critias*, he was probably less interested in conveying information about a lost continent than he was in creating an allegorical situation to make a philosophical and moral point: that even a noble race living under a perfect government could fall into a moral decline and be punished by the gods for their transgressions.

The seekers at Santorini found that the island supported at least one prosperous Minoan settlement that was destroyed in a volcanic explosion. Even considering the alleged error in translation that made Atlantis seem ten times larger than it really was, could the tragic loss of one city on Santorini really have inspired the persistent myth of a mighty nation of sea kings? Professor Galanopoulos says yes.

The various expeditions to Santorini-Thera discovered a wide moat under 1,300 feet of water. Dr. Galanopoulos told *The New York Times*: "Plato, who gave the fullest description of Atlantis, wrote that the hill that stood in the center of the metropolis island was surrounded by a moat which served as a secure harbor. This moat, which encircled the acropolis of the Metropolis, was one of Atlantis' main features. This discovery is one of the most convincing proofs that the legendary Atlantis has been located."

Dr. Galanopoulos goes on to state that Plato described Atlantis as a major sea power where sacred bulls roamed about unhindered. The Minoans who settled Santorini were also a great maritime power and the cult of the bull was a major element in their religious observances.

To the Greek seismologist, Plato's designation of Atlantis as a fortified hill city protected by alternate rings of land and water is but a fanciful description of what Santorini must have looked like before the violent eruption.

To read James Mavor's *Voyage to Atlantis* is to become enthralled by the telling of a scientific adventure story. No one can dispute the importance of the underwater discovery at Santorini-Thera, but this author wonders if the forgotten Minoan town, which covered about half a square mile, could really have become the mythical Atlantis, even if that ancient Greek translator did inadvertently multiply every dimension by ten.

And the legend, as retold by Plato, specifically places the great sea power in the Atlantic, beyond the Pillars of Hercules (Strait of Gibraltar). Why would the ancient storytellers have felt the need to move the location of the city-state from the Aegean to the more distant Atlantic? And why, as the Thera researchers believe, would the Egyptians refer to the Minoan culture as Atlantis? Mavor writes with enthusiasm about the importance of the findings at Thera, but those who have made a study of the Atlantean problem may prefer to echo the words of that popular song by the British folksinger, Donovan, which tell of a great continent lying beneath the Atlantic Ocean.

Strange Discoveries That Upset the Calendar of Time

If one is simply intrigued by lost civilizations of incredibly impressive magnitude, they are being dug up all over the globe in abundance, a fact that will surely begin to push the old, standard calendars into academic attics of unused measuring sticks.

In 1965, while examining the ruins of the Starcevo settlements, a Neolithic civilization first identified in the early 1930s, Yugoslav archaeologist Draodlav Srejovic found round-eyed household dieties of a much older civilization. The dig, situated on the banks of the Danube River about 60 miles from Belgrade, has produced implements which date back to 7000 B.C. The complex layout of the ancient town and the artifacts discovered indicate that the prehistoric peoples were quite advanced as craftsmen and were artistic and religious people as well. But who were they?

In the early 1950s, Dr. J. Louis Giddings, Jr., of the University of Pennsylvania, conducted a study of ancient Arctic ruins that produced evidence of a culture that had circled the entire top of the world in prehistoric times. After an expedition to Northern Canada, Dr. Giddings brought back grooving tools and side blades of a distinctive type that were once believed to be peculiar to Europe and Siberia.

In 1959, Arizona State University students digging in a cave in Camelback Mountain found remains thought to be thousands of years old. In the top layers of the excavation, many centuries old, the diggers found dozens of bundles of reed cigarettes packed in salt. Each bundle was packed in multiples of four, and the cigarettes were fashioned with a perforated reed joint above the tobacco. Filter-tipped cigarettes are obviously nothing new.

When archaeologists opened the tomb of a Celtic princess dated about 600 B.C. near Dijon, France, in the early 1950s, they found that they had pried open a most remarkable enigma as well. Within the tomb stood the wood and wicker carriage of a horse-drawn chariot decorated with perforated bronze. The remains of the princess lay in the carriage, bedecked with exquisite jewelry.

But the puzzle lay in the discovery of a hammered bronze Grecian vase and two cups with black figures known to have been manufactured in the Athens of about 530 B.C. How, the archaeologists pondered, did a Celtic princess in a remote corner of northern Burgundy come to possess works of art that an Athenian king would have given a fortune to possess? And why would a woman be buried in a war chariot?

One archaeologist dared to suggest that the princess might have been a warrior chieftain of the legendary Amazons, against whom the ancient Greeks and Trojans defended themselves.

The myths say the Amazons originated in the Caucasus and eventually settled on the Thermodon River in what is today northern Turkey. The warrior women extended their battle lines as far west as Egypt and as far east as India, declaring truces only long enough to mingle sexually with men of other tribes in order to avoid tribal extinction. Boy children were either sacrificed or returned to their fathers. Girl children were kept and trained in the martial sciences.

In 1965 Moscow radio reported: "One of the most ancient historical legends has been confirmed. The Amazons existed and lived on the territory of our country."

Ukrainian archaeologists discovered ancient Scythian tombs of warrior women near Borispol and Nikopol in the east-central Ukraine. Gold ornaments were found alongside the remains, as well as iron spears, sheaves of arrows, armor, and javelins.

The party propagandists undoubtedly made much of the fact that the very prototype of the super-women had once lived on what is now Soviet soil, and they probably urged their laboring women to emulate the strength, but not the misanthropy, of their fierce predecessors.

Echoes of Atlantis Are Everywhere

This author hopes that he is not emulating the techniques of the propagandist when he points out that yet another "myth" has been tried and found not wanting, but, on the contrary, replete with physical evidence to carve its bold niche in reality. The myth of Atlantis has become one of the most persistent of all legends, and echoes of the destruction of that once-great nation seem to be echoed in the folklore of nearly every people.

Was there a physical Atlantis, a highly evolved society that colonized the world, charted its continent's boundaries, and left remnants of its culture scattered throughout the planet in an epoch before our own?

Is civilization cyclical? Does an Atlantis rise, flower, and get suddenly crushed to dust so that its scattered survivors may start the cycle once again, the golden day of glory but confused memories in their frightened and bewildered brains?

In 1960, Dr. Juan Armenta Comacho, director of the Department of Anthropology at the University of Puebla in Mexico, dug a piece of a mastodon's pelvic bone out of the desert soil at Balsequello, 60 miles southeast of Mexico City. Excavators in the Americas are often unearthing mastodon bones, and such a find is no longer cause for excitement. There must have been a great many mastodons lumbering about the continent at one time. The bit of bone discovered by Dr. Comacho was quite unique, however. On its surface some prehistoric artist had engraved the images of a horse, a camel, a reptile, and a type of mastodon thought to have been extinct for 100,000 years.

Dr. H. Marie Wormington, curator of archaeology at the Denver Museum of Natural History, stated that the artwork and the bone were contemporary. The carving could only have been done on fresh bone, Dr. Wormington commented, not fossil bone.

Just a few short years ago the majority of textbooks taught that man quite probably did not arrive in the Americas until some adventurous Asiatics crossed the Bering land bridge at about the time of Christ. A minority of daring anthropologists were prepared to state that man may have been in the Americas by 3000 B.C., but few academic anthropologists or archaeologists were foolhardy enough to suggest that man may have been in the New World as early as 8000 B.C.

And now the poor scholars are being asked to deal with a bit of mastodon bone that some anonymous artist carved upon at least 100,000 years ago, shortly after the gigantic tusked beast had been freshly killed.

There is an out, but it is certainly one that no orthodox academician who values his professional standing will take. The hunters and the artist could have been on a map-making expedition, as they charted yet another acquisition of their far-reaching Atlantean empire. There were no primitive hunters yet foraging in the Americas; there were no precocious artisans carving on bone; there were only explorers from a mighty nation of sea kings, whose once great continent now lies beneath the Atlantic Ocean.

II

Ancient Sea Kings, Artisans, And Explorers

In the late 1950s, antique dealer R. J. Wills of Monroe, Louisiana, purchased a limestone slab Indian artifact in Cripple Creek, Colorado. The slab had a great many markings on it, and Wills was uncertain if he had really purchased a genuine relic, but he decided to keep it as a curio. It was not until sometime in 1968 that a report of the slab reached Mr. and Mrs. Jack McGee, amateur archaeologists from Fort Worth, Texas. The McGees contacted Wills, and the cooperative antique dealer drove 400 miles to Forth Worth with the enigmatic stone.

According to the *Newsletter*, Vol. 3 No. 3, of the New England Antiquities Research Association: "The McGees promptly saw that the six-line inscription on the rock, measuring 11 x 14 inches, and 4½ inches thick, was in some Old World script, but they mistakenly thought it might be in 4th century Gothic — an ancestral form of Runic, derived from the Greek"

They called for assistance from Professor Vincent Cassidy at the University of Southwestern Louisiana, a member of the NEARA, who told them that the inscription was written in an early variant of modern Greek. Professor Cassidy translated the text with three possible variants: "Here lies the servant of God, Palladeis"; "Here I slew (or sacrificed, or stretched out) the slave of the god Palladeis"; "I, Palladeis, slew the slave of the god."

AMERICAN GEOLOGIST, 1889

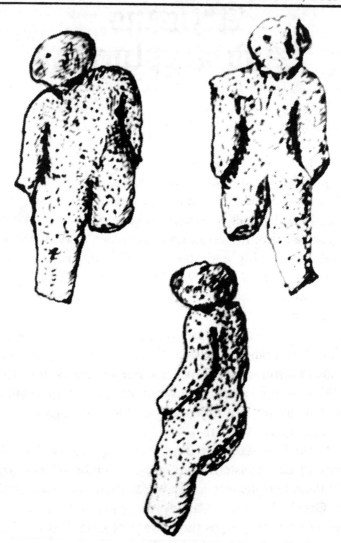

In August, 1889, near Nampa, Idaho, M.A. Kurtz picked up an odd-looking lump of soil that released what appeared to be a tiny human figurine made of clay. Because the controversial object was brought up from a depth of 300 feet during a well-drilling operation, the "Nampa Image" would have to be of vast antiquity.

Professor Cassidy suggests that an inexperienced or semi-literate carver could have produced so grotesquely corrupt an inscription, even within the last century. "White Settlement in Colorado goes back to the 1850s," the NEARA *Newsletter* states. "The possibility, nevertheless, is apparent, that the inscription could be pre-Christian, and relates to some pagan sacrifice, the formula of which has survived in the Greek Orthodox burial phrasing,"

How such a pre-Christian Greek carving could have reached Colorado presents a fascinating mystery that such researchers and scholars as the NEARA are pledged to solve.

Discovering Prehistoric Artifacts in America

Dr. Douglas Schwartz, director of the University of Kentucky Museum of Anthropology found himself with a problem of similar vexation. While digging in a prehistoric Indian site near Eddyville, Kentucky, during the summer of 1959, Schwartz's party unearthed Indian skeletons, pottery, flint knives, and *an iron fork with two rusted tines and a bone handle.*

Indians did not possess iron utensils and forks were unknown to them, so an iron fork really has no business being buried in the site, which dates back to as early as 1200 A.D. Compelled to offer an explanation, Dr. Schwartz came up with one he admitted was pretty weak: a traveler passed by the site years after it had been abandoned and dropped his fork into the ash pit.

In March, 1964, Frank McNamara, Jr., set out to plug a leak in his basement and ended up by pulling out the plug on another perplexing mystery. As McNamara dug in his cellar in South Boston, he uncovered a sculptured ten-pound stone head. The artwork shows the hair in short curls, the eyes slanting downward and quite long, and a rather primitive treatment of the ears.

McNamara's strange find has puzzled some of the best archaeologists at Harvard and a number of museums and schools. Although everyone agrees that the sculpture is not native to America, no one is quite certain if they should ascribe it to the Near

East, Africa, Western Asia, or Egypt. One authority suggested that the primitive head belongs to the Near East of about 700 B.C. The carbon-14 method of determining age can be applied only to organic materials such as bone, wood, coal, and textiles. Stone or pottery artifacts by themselves cannot be carbon-dated, so it is anyone's guess just how old the sculpture really is. The head's place of origin is also a mystery. Was it brought here by prehistoric travelers? Or was a prehistoric culture capable of producing such indigenous artworks?

A Chinese God Unearthed in Oklahoma

As she watched workmen digging a well on the farm of her late husband in Guthrie, Oklahoma, Mrs. Alleyne K. Ecker noticed a peculiar piece of wood protruding from the red clay 15 feet down at the bottom of the pit. Curious, she went down into the well, and pulled the object from the clay.

"After she had washed off the mud and clay that clung to it, she saw that it as a figurine of some eight inches high," writes Frank Volkmann in the December, 1955, issue of *Fate* magazine. "It depicted a bearded, robed and saintly-looking figure holding a lamb in its arms. Even to her untrained eyes it appeared to be very old."

Mrs. Ecker said later that she thought the figurine represented Moses or Abraham or some saint. She showed the object to many people, but none could identify the personage depicted in wood. A man who claimed to have made a study of woodcarving told her that the figure had been shaped from a tree harder than ebony, now extinct for centuries.

Two Chinese students at a nearby college identified the object as an idol of the Chinese god of longevity, Shou Hsing. The figurine was considered to be the earliest representation of the god, who was held in esteem as a deity several centuries before Christ.

According to Volkmann's article, the figurine was found in a type of earth stratum that does not undergo change in a short period of time. Mrs. Ecker has appealed to, and cooperated with, a number of institutions in an effort to answer such questions as how the idol came to America and who brought it here. Throughout the years, she has received several letters from others who claim to have unearthed similar figurines.

The Remarkable Nampa Image

In August, 1889, near Nampa, Idaho, Mr. M.A. Kurtz picked up an odd-looking lump of clay that had been brought up from a depth of 300 feet during a well drilling operation. When he broke it open, he discovered what appeared to be a tiny human figure made of clay. The controversy over the apparent antiquity of the Nampa Image has raged ever since. If the radioactive carbon technique for determining age could be applied to nonorganic materials, perhaps the mystery would be solved, only to present an even deeper, more controversial enigma.

An Assyrian Tablet in the Susquehanna

For 37 years Elwood D. Hummel kept a little rock with strange markings on it in his private collection of curios. He had picked the thing up one day when he was fishing along the Susquehanna River near Winfield, Pennsylvania.

Eventually one of his four kids got hold of it and used it for a plaything. The more the kids played with it, the more pronounced the markings on the surface of the clay object seemed to become.

In 1956, Hummel got curious enough about his find to send it to the curator of a Chicago museum. To his surprise, he received word that the markings on the clay tablet were a cuneiform inscription, which, when translated, described a short-term loan of an Assyrian merchant in Cappadocia around 1900-1800 B.C. No theory was forthcoming about how the record of such a transaction found its way to the bottom of a Pennsylvania river.

Who Discovered America?

Dr. Cyrus Gordon, professor at Brandeis University, believes that such idols, sculptured heads, and figurines are evidence of prehistoric New World migrations of the Scandinavians, Mediterraneans, Negroes, and Japanese. Dr. Gordon recently deciphered a stone tablet that had been found in Columbus, Georgia, in 1968. Dr. Gordon says the tablet tells of a people called the Yuchi who originated in Europe and moved across the southern United States from the Gulf of Mexico. The deciphered stone bears signs identical with certain of those found on Aztec and Minoan tablets, according to the scholar.

The Yuchi's descendants live today in Oklahoma as a tribe of "American Indians" and still celebrate an ancient festival that Dr. Gordon says is described in exact detail in the twenty-third chapter of Leviticus in the Old Testament, a lengthy chapter that delineates the Passover ritual and a harvest ritual, among many others.

For years now, a number of scholars and theorists have insisted that previous research tends to denigrate the maritime ability of the ancients. Dr. Cyrus Gordon is certainly not alone in his belief that the New World was reached by many races long before the Vikings and Columbus, and quite probably before the birth of Christ.

One school of thought champions the Phoenicians as the first discoverers of America. There are the peculiarly Phoenician-like inscriptions found in lost cities in the Matto Grosso, the proto-Phoenician hieroglyphics found in the caves of the Canary Islands, and the Semitic figurines found near Mexico City, the Ecuador coast, and San Miguel de Allende, Mexico.

Dr. Arturo Posnansky stated in the *American Weekly* in 1945 that agri beads had been found embedded in the flesh of Incan mummies. The secret of the manufacture of these beads was known only to the Phoenicians, and since the Incas did not even know how to produce ordinary glass, there seems little chance that they could have made agri beads.

Dr. Posnansky, former president of the Geographical Society of La Paz, Bolivia, commented: "It would have been no particular feat for the Phoenicians to have reached America. Anyone who could sail the Mediterranean, with its sudden and violent storms, could have crossed any ocean."

If one chooses to eliminate the possibility of Atlantis having been a common source for the architecture and customs of the Egyptians and the early Americans, then, almost by default, one has to be open-minded toward an extensive cultural intercourse between the two continents. The Egyptians, as well as the early Central and South Americans, have always been considered virtual land-lubbers compared to other ancient peoples, but the circumstantial evidence certainly exists in abundance that, if they did not borrow from a common culture, one or the other of them managed to breach the great ocean which separated them.

Most obvious are the pyramids common to both Egypt and South America. The South American pyramids were usually flattened with a temple on top, and many of the American structures house just as elaborate burials as those given the Pharaohs.

Both peoples practiced the mysterious art of mummification. Author Lewis Spence tells us that in America the internal organs were buried separately from the bodies, in four canopic jars, closely resembling those used in Egypt. Each jar lid represented the head of a god, just as the canopic jars in Egypt portrayed the four sons of Horus, gods of the four winds. The color of the jar representing each deity and the organ assigned to each correspond almost exactly in the two cultures.

Children of the Red One

Some scholars such as Dr. Rendel Harris have used philology as a method of detecting cultural origin. Peru, for example, may suggest "per-or," the Great House, one of the early titles which later became the word "Pharaoh." Niagara can be seen as "Ngara," the Bull of Ra,

Native American petroglyphs — "rock writing" — may reveal clues to a world before our own.

a name sometimes applied to the Nile River. Massachusetts might be translated as the Egyptian, Children of the Red One. (Both the Egyptians and the Atlanteans were known to be proud of their reddish complexions.) Tennessee is the "land of Isis." Guatemala is the Spanish version of the Indian name *Wa-Te-Ra,* which certain scholars have said is pure Egyptian for "Way of the Setting Sun." Campeche Bay, north of Tabasco, comes from *Kham,* the oldest name for Egypt, and *petche,* a curving body of water. Literally, then, Campeche Bay means "Bay of Egypt." The river Nil (Nile) is found in Guatemala, and the ruins of pyramids dot its banks.

Other theorists build strong cases for expeditions of Minoans, Jews, Irish, Etruscans, Romans, Frisians, Chinese, and Sumerians having reached the New World in ancient times. It may well have been that all these peoples did, indeed, reach the American shores thousands of years before the Vikings and, later, Columbus braved the terrors and privations of an ocean crossing. But a mysterious kind of rock writing with identical inscriptions found from Egypt to California, from Ireland to Iran, indicates that an unknown race roamed the world in prehistory.

The Stone Writers

When the first white settlers entered the Blue Ridge Mountain country of western North Carolina, they found, in what is today Jackson County, a large rock covered with peculiar inscriptions. The Cherokee Indians, whose land the settlers were invading, could not explain the big rocks with funny scratchings. Whoever had scribbled on the rock had done so long before the Indians entered North Carolina.

In 1961, Dr. Gerald Smith, a museum director, told the San Bernardino, California, *Daily Sun* that the rock carvings, called petroglyphs, vary greatly in age.

"Some of the newer petroglyphs are frankly little more than doodling, but others contain definitely known designs and directions toward water," Dr. Smith said. "Present day Indians appear to have lost, or never known, the meaning of many figures that appear in many carvings. Similarity of some designs to letters of the Phoenicians and Sanskrit alphabets has given rise to theories that some of the older writings were done by prehistoric wanderers from the Old World."

In other words, a party of explorers from some undetermined prehistoric culture could have left inscriptions that, over the years, more sensitive Indians had tried to trace or imitate. One can, therefore, either rush to support those who claim the Phoenicians found their way from the eastern side of the Mediterranean to the western coast of America, or one can hold out for an earlier people, from whom the Phoenicians borrowed, or learned, many of the characters of their alphabet. The safest theory of all, of course, is to maintain that the petroglyphs are decorative Amerindian rock carvings.

William Coxon and his wife Mae Marie, amateur archaeologists, spent years studying the petroglyphs of the ancient Stone-Writers, whom they believe the people of antiquity called "The Cyclops." In an article in the February, 1959 issue of *Fate* magazine, William Coxon set forth a number of their findings.

"The Stone-Writers wrote geometrically with signs and symbols, and used pictures only to illustrate action or objects. In the strictest application of the word, there is not a pictograph among their rock-writings although there occurs a light sprinkling of ideographs," Coxon said.

The Coxons feel it is likely that the Egyptian scribes were familiar with the signs and symbols left by Stone-Writers along the Upper Nile. It is their contention that geological dating places the Cyclops' exploration of the Nile about 1,500 years before the Egyptians were known to appear there.

"In almost every antiquity everywhere are found geometric designs influenced and accounted for by the symbolism of the Stone-Writers," Coxon continued in the article.

"The geometric writings of the Stone-Writers are. . .older by thousands of years than the Egyptian carvings and instead of being confined to a limited area of the earth's surface, they are world-wide. Decoding them will not only permit our generation to delve deeper into antiquity, it may possibly bring about a reconstruction of world prehistory."

The Coxons state that by comparing, paralleling, and counter-parting geometric signs, symbols, and sequences, they had, at the time of that writing, noted a total of 241 sequences of symbols used throughout the world. The Stone-Writers used 201, the Eastern world trailed with 171 sequences, and the two hemispheres share 131 sequences.

Judging by the height of the rock writing above the terrain, the Coxons believe the Stone-Writers to have been about the same size as the average human being of today. They are convinced, however, that they must have possessed greater strength and endurance to have enabled them to negotiate the wild rivers and wilderness trails.

Some of the rock carvings show men dressed in short kilts which come to a point between knee and hip. The Coxons feel that such garb is identical to that worn by the dynastic Egyptian laborers. A carving of a fully dressed man depicts a loose-fitting garment reaching to the knees.

The Coxons were convinced by their study that the Stone-Writers were not merely hunters or nomads, but an intelligent people, thorough and systematic in all that they did. "Method, regularity, and repetition of written characters cannot be associated with savages," they aver. "They are the result of thought, necessity, and trained mentality."

In summation, the Coxons concluded that they had developed the evidence for an intelligent, prehistoric culture which had ranged the whole world. "They traveled the oceans, or at least the coastlines, and they penetrated far up into the continents along the rivers . . . Along the stream, lake, and ocean shores, they left guide signs to mark the way for others who followed them. . . ."

But the irritating question remains to haunt us: who followed them, and who were *they*?

New Hampshire's Mystery Hill

On September 6, 1969, United Press International carried an announcement by James P. Whittall, Jr., an archaeologist for the New England Antiquities Research Association, stating that the strange stone structures known as Mystery Hill outside of North Salem, New Hampshire, were built by a group of people who may have been of Mediterranean origin. Whittall's radiocarbon tests indicate that the ruins are about 3,000 years old. Artifacts found at the large complex of stone chambers, including tools and pieces of pottery, suggest a culture similar to those of the Mediterranean from about 3000 B.C. to 500 B.C.

Whittall's favorite theory is that the chambers and the shaping of the stones are "strikingly similar" to the Megalithic culture known to have lived on the Iberian peninsula, that is, Spain and Portugal. (As an aside, and this is my conjecture, not Mr. Whittall's, the Basques of Portugal, according to the old legends, were said to be among the survivors of the Atlantean tragedy. Again, could it not be possible that instead of the ancient inhabitants of the Iberian peninsula having made it to New Hampshire, that a source common to both cultures, i.e, Atlantis, may have established colonies in both geographic locations?)

Dr. Stephen Williams, head of the Peabody Museum at Harvard, would not endorse either Whittall's theory or my aside. He believes the structures were erected during the colonial American period, in the seventeenth or eighteenth centuries.

Dr. Ross T. Christensen appraised the Megalithic evidence in New Hampshire in the Society of Early Historic Archaeology's *Newsletter and Proceedings,* January, 1970: "A number of theories have been proposed to explain the origin of this strange complex of 'maverick' archaeology. The constructions were plainly not built by New England Indians or their ancestors of any known variety. They clearly do not fit into the pattern of prehistoric cultural development usually assigned to the Eastern Woodlands area by professional archaeologists. The latter as a rule consider the 'caves' to be stables or root cellars of early New England farmers . . . and indeed they probably were used as such at a later time. . . .

"William B. Goodwin was persuaded that the constructions at Mystery Hill were built by a band of Irish monks fleeing from the Vikings. . . .

"Charles M. Boland believes that Irish monks were later occupants of the site, but that it was the Phoenicians who built it in the first place. . . .

"Frank Glynn, a prominent amateur archaeologist of Clinton, Connecticut, developed a theory that the New England complex is related to the Bronze Age 'Megalithic' culture of Malta and western Mediterranean lands of c. 1500 B.C. . . .

"Adding to the excitement of the C-14 date (1045 B.C.) . . . James P. Whittall, Jr., staff archaeologist of the NEARA . . . traveled to Portugal to examine at close range the Megalithic constructions of that country. . . .

". . . the evidence so far argues in favor of a transatlantic crossing. But apparently those who came were not Indian hunters, Yankee farmers, Irish monks, or Phoenician mariners; they were a nameless people of the late Bronze Age of the western Mediterranean area, perhaps from Portugal."

A personal communication from Andrew E. Rothovius, NEARA historian and editor of the NEARA *Newsletter* clarified a few misconceptions that had been circulated about Mystery Hill in a number of popular publications.

"The twenty-two stone structures are not neatly buried' as has been stated in some reports." he told me. "They are on a bare granite outcropping where there is no soil to bury anything in. The stone carvings often referred to are not on the side of the large stone-grooved slab, but are elsewhere on the site. The gazelle carving shows the entire animal, not just the head, as has been reported. The axe is the Minoan labrys, or double axe, a point of considerable importance. The stone-lined well is more probably an incomplete mining shaft, but it would be highly incorrect to call it a buried cylinder, as certain accounts have had it."

Forgotten Shafts and Mines

Other mysterious shafts in various parts of the country have been found leading to what have been unmistakable mines, producing evidence of forgotten miners of great antiquity.

In 1953, workers of the Lion coal mine of Wattis, Utah, broke into a network of tunnels between five and six feet in height and width, which contained coal of such antiquity that it had weathered to uselessness for any kind of burning or heat. According to a report in the February, 1954, issue of *Coal Age,* a search of the outside of the mountain in direct line with the tunnels revealed no trace of any entrance, but since the tunnels were discovered when the men were working at eight-foot coal seam at 8,500 feet, someone certainly had conducted an ambitious mining project at sometime.

University of Utah professors John E. Wilson of the Department of Engineering and Jesse D. Jennings of the Department of Anthropology examined the tunnels on August 13, 1953, accompanied by Grant Foulger, purchasing agent, and Earle McAlpine, mining engineer.

According to Professor Wilson: "Without doubt, both drifts were man-made. Though no evidence was found at the outcrop, the tunnels apparently were driven 450 feet from the outside to the point where the present workings broke into them . . . There is no visible basis for dating the tunnels. . . ."

Professor Jennings commented that he did not feel that he had observed enough to shape an opinion as to the origin of the ancient miners, but he expressed doubt that the tunnels could have been the work of any American Indian of whom we have any written or archaeological record. "In the first place, such works would have required immediate and local need for coal," he stated.

"It is not reasonable to suppose that extensive tunnels would have been driven to produce coal for export to distant parts . . . because, before the white man came, transport was by human cargo carriers, or porters, and long-distance movement of heavy loads was impracticable," Professor Jennings went on. "As for local use, there was no reported extensive burning of coal by aboriginals in the region of the Wattis mine."

Certainly, we must echo Professor Jennings's admonition when he cautions us that it is not "reasonable" to suppose that some primitive miners drilled such extensive tunnels so that they might export coal. After all, there was no demand for large quantities of coal among early Amerindians, and those few tribes known to have done any mining at all, such as the Hopi Indians in northern Arizona, employed only primitive stripping methods.

By the testimony of the mining engineers, the deep tunnels were of such antiquity that the coal had been oxidized to a worthless state, and there were not only tunnels, but coal mining rooms. The only way that any of this can become "reasonable" is if we consider the possibility of technicians from a highly advanced prehistoric culture, who actually set about seeking coal for their complex civilization and who had the methods of transport necessary to export the coal back to their culture.

A contemporary analogy might be made of the desert tribesman who sits astride horse or camel and watches the great oil wells pumping black fluid into barrels for export to more advanced, faraway civilizations with such strange sounding names as Detroit, Chicago, and St. Louis. The desert tribesman has no use for the black fluid. It cannot quench his animal's thirst nor keep the sun from scorching the sands, but the crazy foreigners are prepared to wage war over the stuff.

So might it have been in remote antiquity. Simple Amerindian tribesmen may have lounged about in primitive smugness as strange, bearded foreigners worked day and night inside a mountain to haul out worthless black rocks.

A similar situation may have existed in the Keweenaw Peninsula and on Isle Royale in Michigan. An estimated two-million pounds of copper were mined on Isle Royale by some unnamed prehistoric mining empire that had the means of transporting the metal out of the immediate area. The principal questions puzzling archaeologists are who the ancient miners were and why they suddenly abandoned their vast operations.

We might suggest that a cataclysm in the seat of their empire may have rendered their continued mining operations impossible. If their homeland were suddenly destroyed, the miners left marooned in the Americas might have gradually become assimilated with the Amerindian tribes in the area. They may have repeated over and over again the tales of their wondrous homeland, the great nation that sank beneath the sea as the result of volcanic explosion or some other natural, or man-made, catastrophe. These stories may exist today in the legends and dances of the Amerindians.

An Iron Pot From A Lump Of Coal

In 1912, two employees of the Municipal Electric Plant, Thomas, Oklahoma, used a sledge to break apart a chunk of coal too large for the furnace. An iron pot toppled from the center of the lump, leaving an impression in the coal. The coal had been mined near Wilburton, Oklahoma, an area of the southwest that seems to yield numerous erratics and anomalous footprints.

The two men freely signed an affidavit attesting to their incredible discovery. The artifact has been photographed and thousands of curious men and women have examined the pot from an unknown time and place.

A Human Tooth Found In Bear Creek Mine

On November 7, 1926, fossil hunters in the coal beds of the Bear Creek Field near Billings, Montana, found a human tooth, the enamel of which had long since turned to carbon and the lime of the roots to iron. According to *The New York Times* for November 8, 1926:

The tooth, declared by dentists of this city [Billings] to be the second lower molar of a human being, was found by Dr. J. C. Siegfriedt of Bear Creek, who has been collecting fossils for the University of Iowa and for other institutions.

The coal deposit is in the fortunian formation, lowest of those laid down in the Eocene Period. Many fossils, including ganoids, a kind of fish scale, and sharks' teeth have been found in the deposit by Dr. Siegfriedt, who asserts that it furnishes prolific material for fossil and dinosaur research.

In 1958, Professor Johannes Hurzeler of the Museum of Natural History in Basel, Switzerland, found the jawbone of a child flattened like a piece of sheet iron in a lump of coal dated from the Miocene age, roughly ten million years ago.

An Ancient Building Buried in a Mine Shaft

In private correspondence, W. W. McCormick of Abilene, Texas, relates his grandfather's account of a building that was buried in a coal mine shaft:

In the year 1928, I, Atlas Almon Mathis, was working in coal mine No. 5, located two miles north of Heavener, Oklahoma. This mine was so deep that they let us down into it on an elevator. . . They pumped air down to us, it was so deep. . . .

. . . One night I shot four shots [referring to blasting coal loose] in room 24 of this mine, and the next morning there were several concrete blocks laying in the room. These blocks were 12-inch cubes and were so smooth and polished on the outside that all six sides could serve as mirrors. Yet they were full of gravel, because I chipped one of them open with my pick, and it was plain concrete inside.

As I started to timber the room up, it caved in; and I barely escaped. When I came back after the cave-in, a solid wall of these polished blocks was left exposed. About 100 to 150 yards farther down our air core, another miner struck this same wall, or one very similar. Immediately they [the mining company officers] pulled us out of this wing of the mine and forbade us to tell anything we had seen.

This mine was closed in the fall of 1928, and the crew went to Kentucky ...

. . . Before I started working on this crew, they had a similar experience in mine 24 at Wilburton, Oklahoma in about the year 1926.

They said they dug up two odd things: One was a solid block of silver in the shape of a barrel, and the other was a bone that was about the size of an elephant's. I don't know if they means only in diameter or in diameter and in length, but they did say it had knuckles on each end. The silver block had the prints of the staves on it, and the saw that first struck it cut off a chip on the edge at one end. The miners saw the silver dust the saw was pulling out and went to dig out the block.

What was done with these things, I do not know. In the case of the blocks in my room in No. 5, I don't think any were kept.

A Human Leg in a West Virginia Coal Mine

A few years ago Dr. Henry Morris, an enthusiastic supporter of the Creationist movement, reported that he had personally interviewed a coal miner in West Virginia who had excavated a perfectly formed human leg that had changed into coal.

He also encountered the claim that miners in the general area of West Virginia had unearthed a well-constructed concrete building.

A Most Incredible Find
at the Big Indian Copper Mine

In May of 1971, while searching for little spheres of blue azurite on a "rockhound" tour of bulldozed land that belonged to a mining company, Lin Ottinger, tour guide and amateur geologist-archaeologist, found trace of human remains in a geological stratum that is approximately 100 million years old.

The find was precipitated when a woman collector handed Ottinger a specimen for identification. He immediately recognized the object as a human tooth.

Ottinger shouted, assembling the group of scattered rockhounds he had brought to the Big Indian Copper Mine in Lisbon Valley, about 35 miles south of Moab, Utah. After he had told the men and women what to look for, Ottinger joined them in a careful, coordinated search of the bulldozed area.

Might it be possible that there could also be bits of bone as well as additional teeth lying half-buried after their rude disinterment by the mining company's bulldozers? Ottinger instructed his rockhounds to look carefully for the telltale brownish stains that decaying organic matter leaves in sand.

In a matter of a few minutes, Ottinger's spontaneously assembled crew had located several more teeth and a number of bone fragments, one of which was quite obviously from a human jawbone.

Then someone gave a triumphant cry of discovery. A trace of brown discolored the white, semi-rock sand.

Ottinger knelt above the dark stain and carefully began probing the decomposing sandstone with his knife blade. With almost surgical skill, Ottinger soon uncovered a smoothly rounded bone that had acquired a greenish hue from the copper in the sandstone.

At this point, the amateur archaeologist demonstrated his professional attitude toward what could be a major find. He stopped digging. He knew that human bones left in place, *in situ*, as he found them in ancient rock strata could present the ax that could topple the current consensus of how long man's family tree had been growing.

If one finds human bones *in situ* in a rock formation, then the skeletal fragments have to be as old as the rock that surrounds them. Of course the very idea of human bones in rock is repellent to the ears of any orthodox scientist, for his dogma declares that the genus

Homo and any of his ancestors is far younger than the very newest rock formations.

Lin Ottinger carefully covered the exposed fragments with moistened paper, then sprinkled the pater with loose sand. He wanted to be certain that the bones would be protected from exposure to the desert air.

Ottinger was well aware of the fact that only an accredited scientist could establish whether or not the bones were truly human and if they were "in place" within the rock, so he notified Dr. W. Lee Stokes, with whom he had worked in previous paleontological finds.

A Human Skeleton 100-Million Years Old

According to the Moah, Utah, *Times Independent* June 3, 1971: "The implications of Ottinger's find were instantly recognized by Dr. Stokes. If the human remains were truly "in place" in the Dakota formation, that is, not washed or fallen in from higher and younger strata, then the remains would have to be the same age as the stratum in which they were found. This would be in the vicinity of 100 million years. . . ."

Dr. Stokes referred the investigation to a colleague, Dr. J. P. Marwitt, professor of anthropology at the University of Utah. A natural history television photography team, a local news reporter, and a number of interested people accompanied Ottinger and Dr. Marwitt to the desert valley site.

Dr. Marwitt immediately set to work uncovering the bones.

"Parts of at least two separate skeletons were exposed in the preliminary survey," reported the *Times Independent.* "While Marwitt and Ottinger were working on the prime site, several volunteers were screening loose sand and dirt in the vicinity for teeth and bone shards. Quite a number were found."

As the skeletons were uncovered, it soon became apparent that they were "in place"and had not been washed in or fallen down from higher strata.

"The portions of skeletons that were exposed were still articulated, that is, were still joined naturally, indicating that the bodies were still intact when buried or covered in the Dakota formation," the *Times Independent* stated.

An interesting side feature of the find was the fact that the bones had been stained a bright green by the copper salts that occur in the vicinity.

"In addition," the *Times Independent* commented, "the dark organic stains found around the bones indicate that the bones had been complete bodies when deposited in the ancient stratum."

Dr. Marwitt pointed out a number of curious aspects of the remarkable find. One of the bodies appeared to be in the position very often used by ancient Indian tribes in their formal burial observances, but the upper body of the other skeleton had been carried away. The bulldozer that had removed the rock and other materials from the site was blamed as the most likely body snatcher.

Mine metallurgist Keith Barrett remembered that the rock and soil that had been above the remains before the bulldozer work had begun had been "continuous . . . with no caves or major faults or crevices visible. Thus, before the mine exploration work, the human remains had been completely covered by about fifteen feet of material, including five or six feet of solid rock. This provided strong, but not conclusive, evidence that the remains are as old as the strata in which they were found."

And, once again, we are speaking of an age of at least 100 million years. Due to a certain local faulting and shifting, the site could be either in the lower Dakota or the still older upper Morrison formation.

Scientists, though, found a serious contradiction inherent in the find. Even though the skeletons were found in rock stratum over 100 million years old, they appeared to be the remains of *Homo sapiens*, modern man, not some ancient, ape-like predecessor.

". . . Even though the rock and soil layers originally above the ones were continuous and unbroken as claimed by mine officials, there is still the possibility, in fact a high probability, that the original

In May of 1971, amateur geologist-archaeologist Lin Ottinger found traces of Homo sapiens remains in a geological stratum indicative of 100 million years old. The incredible discovery was made at the Big Indian Copper Mine in Lisbon Valley, about 25 miles south of Moab, Utah.

owners of the bones had simply been using a narrow cave in the Dakota formation, when it collapsed and buried them, then later filled in solid with the sandy soil that surrounded the bones when they were found," stated the *Times Independent* in summation of the scientist's position.

Laboratory age-dating seemed to be the only method of resolving the mystery presented by the human bones in rock, ostensibly over 100 million years old. Dr. Marwitt removed the skeletal fragments and transported them to his university's laboratories.

And it is here, according to F. A. Barnes's article in the February, 1975 issue of *Desert* magazine, that the matter rested:

"Somehow, the university scientists never got around to age-dating the mystery bones. Dr. Marwitt seemed to lose interest . . . then transferred to an eastern university. No one else took over the investigation. Lin Ottinger, growing tired of waiting after more than a year, reclaimed his box of bones.

". . . It is highly probable that the bones are, indeed, this old. Yet, who knows? Without that vital age-dating, no one can say positively that they are not . . . .

"Part of the mystery, of course, is why the University of Utah scientists chose not to age-date the . . . bones and clear up at least the question of their actual age.

"And so the mystery remains, perhaps never to be solved."

The Imprint of a Shoe Sole 80 Million Years Old

And when will we be able to stamp "solved" across the dossier that contains the data concerning the discovery made on January 25, 1927 in Nevada of a shoe sole that was fossilized in Triassic limestone, thereby placing man back in the times of the giant reptiles? In the late 1920s, the Oakland Museum in California published a small bulletin under the title "The Doheny Scientific Expedition to the Hava Supai Canyon, Northern Arizona."

A Mr. Knapp, the discoverer of the erratic, writes that the fossil lay among some loose rocks. He picked it up and, upon later examination, "came to the conclusion that it is a layer from the heel of a shoe which had been pulled from the balance of the heel by suction; the rock being in a plastic state at that time. I found it in limestone of the Triassic Period, a belt of which runs through that section of the hills."

The relic was taken to New York where it was analyzed by a competent geologist of the Rockefeller Foundation, who verified Mr. Knapp's assessment and pronounced the fossil as unquestionably formed in Triassic limestone.

Excerpting from the Oakland Museum's bulletin:

> Micro-photographs were made which showed very clearly that it bore a minute resemblance to a well-made piece of leather, stitched by hand, and at one time worn by a human foot. The photographs showed the stitches very plainly; at one place it was double-stitched and the twist of the thread could be clearly seen. The thread is smaller than any used by shoemakers of today. Minute crystals of sulphide of mercury are to be noticed throughout the spaces of this fossil shoe sole, these minerals having been deposited in the long ago by waters which carried them in solution.

Samuel Hubbard, honorary curator of archaeology of the Oakland Museum, is quoted as saying: "There are whole races of primitive men on earth today, utterly incapable of etching that picture or sewing that moccasin. What becomes of the Darwinian Theory in the face of this evidence that there were intelligent men on earth millions of years before apes are supposed to have evolved?"

The White Sands Giants

The White Sands National Museum near Alamogordo, New Mexico, contains some 176,000 acres of white alabaster. Geologists theorize that this gypsum was precipitated as arid winds dried up an inland sea. Somewhere in the great expanse of gypsum are what appear to be the sandal prints of some prehistoric human giant, who could only have made such impressions when the muddy sediment of the primeval ocean was beginning to harden.

In the *Story of the Great White Sands*, a booklet distributed at the National Monument, an account is related concerning the discovery of the massive human tracks:

> In the fall of 1932, Ellis Wright, a government trapper, reported that he had found human tracks of unbelievable size imprinted in the gypsum rock on the west side of White Sands. At his suggestion a party was made up to investigate. Mr. Wright served as guide....
>
> As Mr. Wright reported, there were thirteen human tracks crossing a narrow swag, pretty well out between the mountains and the sands. Each track was approximately 22 inches long and from eight-to-ten inches wide. It was the consensus that the tracks were made by a human being, for the print was perfect, and even the instep plainly marked. However, there was no one in the group who cared to venture a guess as to when the tracks were made, or how they came to be of their tremendous size. It is one of the great unsolved mysteries of the Great White Sands.

The Apache Crown Dance

According to L. Taylor Hansen, the movements of the Mescallero (Apache) Crown Dance and the costume worn during its performance offer indisputable evidence of the ancient Atlantean heritage of certain American tribes. "The Crown Dance costume includes the golden-fringed warsheath of ancient Atlantis, the black boots of the calf and the star symbol and short swords of the warriors of that forgotten land, and the Crown of the Trident, the symbol of the royal house of Atlantis," editorialized Ray Palmer in his November, 1966, issue of *Search* magazine.

"Atlantis was the land of the trident," he goes on. "The trident was the symbol of ancient Atlantis, and its three prongs pointed upward. Today the American Indians dances the Crown dance and the Dance of the Trident, and when he turns the prongs down, he is saying: 'I remember the old Red Land of my forefathers, and how it sank beneath the sea.' In the dance, the dancers enter from the east — the direction of the Lost Land under the Sunrise Sea, the Indian name for the Atlantic."

Vestiges of Atlantis may also exist in man's universal unconscious, his dreams, and even in his inspired visions. Edgar Cayce was one man who lay in trance and relayed an enormous amount of material about the lost land of prehistory which we have come to call Atlantis. As if the Atlantean Problem were not crowded and confused enough, Cayce introduced elements into the chaotic kettle of controversy which were at once metaphysical and technological. Cayce's vision of Atlantis was that of a mighty nation of super science caught in the all-entwining web of the ageless power struggle between good and evil.

III

Edgar Cayce's Vision Of A Dying Nation

Edgar Cayce is thought by many to have been the greatest clairvoyant and prophet since the days of apostolic revelation. Although the testimony of Cayce's numerous medical readings remains available for examination by the most persistent skeptic, his entranced pronouncements of clients' past lives have not been substantiated by any evidence other than the subjective appraisals of those men and women who sought out the sleeping prophet.

The same state of affairs exists with Cayce's many trance statements on Atlantis. Since Cayce was so accurate in his medical readings—some believers argue—it stands to reason that he should also be accurate in his vision of a fantastic world of uneclipsed scientific technology caught in a primeval struggle between the forces of good and evil. As yet, of course, no physical evidence exists that such a land of super science ever existed in a continent situated in the Atlantic. If, however, certain of the seer's predictions should be realized, and Atlantis should rise as he foretold, the name of Edgar Cayce will surely be carved in stone for all future generations to revere.

But our purpose in this chapter is not to assess the merits of Edgar Cayce. Rather, let us present a portrait of the Atlantis he envisioned, a Atlantis being slowly rent asunder by its own super science gone mad.

Cayce depicted the panorama of Atlantis in over 650 life readings given over a period of 21 years. During that span of time the information he imparted was amazingly consistent. Never once did he confuse a date or jumble events he had ascribed to a particular era in Atlantean history in readings given years before.

Cayce's history of Atlantis is conveniently divided into three broad eras: the First Destruction, the Second Destruction, and the Third, or Final, Destruction. Students of the Atlantis readings have placed the time of the First Destruction at approximately 50,000 B.C. At this time Atlantis was a continent, and the seismographic disturbances were minor compared to what was eventually to come. The Second Destruction was more violent, succeeding in breaking up the land mass into five major islands, about 28,000 B.C. The Final Destruction of Atlantis, which plunged the mighty civilization beneath the waves, occurred around 10,000 B.C.

Cayce's elaborations on how the physical body of the species *Homo sapiens* came into being neatly excuse him from the necessity of presenting fossil remains to validate his point. Consistent with the first chapter in Genesis, Cayce declared that physical life was already pursuing its evolutionary path on this planet before the arrival of man. Furthermore, when man first appeared here, he was in soul form, rather than sheathed in a physical body. Free from the limitations of a material form, these Souls were capable of projecting themselves into other forms of life. They could inhabit a plant, the trunk of a tree, or the body of an animal.

The purpose of the soul in entering these material forms was to experience creation, which, being a spiritual entity, it could not do without the medium of physical senses. In fact, Cayce declared that the five races of man occurred simultaneously upon Earth because that number represents the five senses, or the five attributes, through which physical and spiritual consciousness may be bridged.

The Origin of the Red Race

Atlantis embodied the red race. According to the readings, these people developed at a much more rapid rate than the other four races. The Souls that projected into the Atlantean land were quicker at learning how to manipulate the forces manifest in their surroundings, and how to develop them.

In appearance, Cayce described them as being ". . . rather of the nature of thought forms, or able to push themselves in that direction in which their development took shape in thought — much in the way and manner as the amoeba would in the waters of a stagnant bay, or lake, in the present. As these took form by the gratifying of their own desire for that which builded or added to the material conditions, they became hardened or set — much in the form of the existent human body of the day" (364.4).

What Cayce is saying here is that these Souls, by endlessly and carelessly projecting themselves into matter, eventually found their ability to project *out* of matter waning. Gradually, materiality hardened around these Souls, and they found themselves caught fast in a physical form.

The Division of the Sexes

Occurring at the same time was the division of the sexes. According to Cayce's entranced teaching, the Soul is androgynous — that is, it incorporates both the male and female principles. It was in Atlantis, therefore, if Cayce is to be believed, that sex came into being, due to the separation of these two principles.

The combination of projection into animal forms and the arrival of sex produced some strange bedfellows. The offspring of these unions were frequently grotesque mixtures of human and animal traits. There were great differences of opinion concerning the nature of these "things," as they were called. The "things" remained a central issue throughout the history of Atlantis, dividing the two rival groups that soon developed.

Children of the Law of One

The struggle between the Children of the Law of One and the Sons of Belial continued throughout the successive destructions of

Atlantis. The final destruction was the result of actions taken by the Sons of Belial, who destroyed themselves as well as their enemies with their insatiable desire for knowledge and power.

The beginnings of this classic struggle between good and evil date back to that primeval time when Souls split into two separate sexes and took on physical embodiment. The readings indicate that the material encasement of Souls was the result of self-indulgence and self-aggrandizement on the part of the Souls. Through misuse of their creative powers and by interrupted the evolutionary pattern of the planet, they were now made subject to its laws. They would live in a physical body until that body's natural death.

Souls in this position were so blinded by their own selfishness that they cut themselves off equally from their spiritual nature and their Creator. Those who were still pure in their descent, however (the Children of the Law of One), had compassion for the trapped Sons of Belial and attempted to provide a vehicle — man — through which Souls could again realize their divine nature and regain their spiritual heritage.

Thus the entranced Cayce explained the physical body of man, and laid the groundwork for the doctrine of reincarnation. Concurrently, the basis for the continuance of Atlantean civilization was established.

The Sons of Belial

The Sons of Belial, off to a bad start, continued to blacken their record. As stated earlier, the red-skinned Atlanteans were described as more facile in thought and manipulation than the other races developing on the planet. Cayce's further elaborations of this point boggles the minds of those who assume we are the descendants of a stone age mentality, for he stated under trance that Atlantis before 50,000 B.C. was adept in communications, heavier-than-air machines, and radioactive forces. The "electrical forces" of nature, as he called them, were harnessed, and the natural gases of the earth's interior were utilized. All these forces, however, were developed for destructive purposes.

The perniciousness of these inventions was what caused the First Destruction of Atlantis, the readings inform us. The interference with inner-earth gas resources and the misuse of natural electricity caused volcanic eruptions in the land. The violent earthquakes and volcanic blasts of the First Destruction, though, were only the distant rumblings of the even greater catastrophe which would eventually befall the island continent.

Dating from the First Destruction, the population of Atlantis divided itself into two camps. Reading 877-26 tells us that the Sons of Belial strove only for ". . . the gratifying, the satisfying, the use of material things for self, without thought or consideration as to the sources of such nor the hardships in the experience of others. Or, in other words, as we would term it today, they were those without a standard of morality.

"The Sons of Belial had no standard, save of self-aggrandizement."

The same reading, given May 23, 1938, details the other side—the Children of the Law of One—as believing:

"The soul was given by the Creator or entered from outside sources into the projection of the mental and spiritual self at the given periods. That was the standard of the Law of One, but was rejected by the Sons of Belial."

This almost allegorical separation in beliefs arose over the application of certain physical laws. Today's practitioners and students of the occult generally regard both spiritual and physical laws to be neutral. Their positive or negative values are ascribed to them according to the way in which they are used by mankind. The typical example is the splitting of the atom which can provide tremendous power resources to impoverished areas when in the hands of ethically motivated people, but which can utterly destroy the same regions when in the hands of a military system that values expedience over human life.

It was precisely this position—having to decide whether or not to put a positive or a negative value on a harnessed power source—

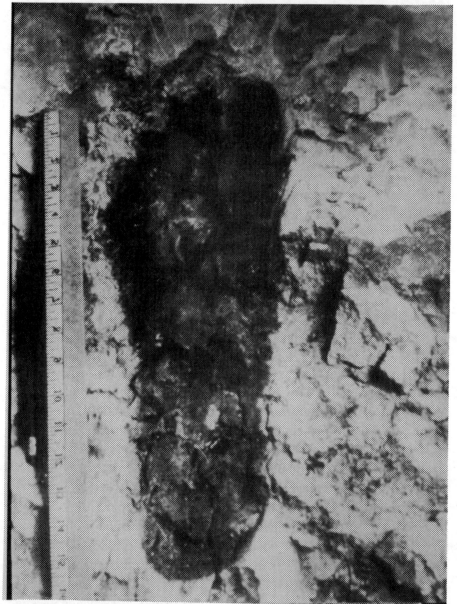

Dr. Clifford Burdick has spent more than 20 years in a study of what appears to be human footprints in strata contemporaneous with dinosaur tracks. Such discoveries, if proven to be authentic, will totally revolutionize the academically accepted time table of human evolution.

in which the Atlanteans found themselves. Numerous readings touch upon this moral predicament, some delving more deeply into the subject than others.

And it is at this point in Cayce's account of Atlantean history that parallels to America begin most noticeably to appear. The parallels grow increasingly obvious as this country's technological growth abounds, and they abruptly cease just short of the deadly debacle that sealed Atlantis's fate. It was Cayce's belief propounded in the unconscious state, that even as individual Souls reincarnated, so did groups of Souls. And, even as a single entity incurs a Karmic debt, so does a nation. All must pay for deeds perpetrated against others, and they must be repaid in like measure. With this in mind, let us return once more to the Sons of Belial and the Children of the Law of One.

The First Destruction

The time leading up to the First Destruction was characterized by violent disagreement between these two opposing philosophies of life over the nature of the "things." While the Sons of Belial enslaved these hapless creatures, making them little better than robots or automatons, the Children of the Law of One taught that these beings were not objects, but imprisoned Souls containing the divine spark of their Creator. As such they were to be helped out of their miserable existence, not kept there for purposes of exploitation. This difference in attitude and treatment of the "things" persisted all the way up to the Final Destruction.

Following the first breaking up of portions of Atlantis, referred to by the sleeping prophet as the First Destruction, the war continued to rage between the two opposing forces. Scientific and technological advances spiraled. The Atlanteans took a liking to convenience inventions — devices that would lighten their work load.

The Death Ray

One of these devices that was further developed was the so-called Death Ray, or "super-cosmic ray." The reading describing this Death Ray was given February 21, 1933. At that time Edgar Cayce also stated that the same death ray would be rediscovered within the next twenty-five years. A twenty-five year span from 1933 brings one to the year 1958. By that time the antineutron had been established, opening the door to antimatter theorems. When antimatter comes into contact with ordinary matter, the entire antimatter mass is transformed into energy. This energy exceeds the output of nuclear fission and fusion, wherein only a small fraction of the mass is converted to energy.

The year 1958 also saw development of the maser (*M*icrowave *A*mplification by *S*timulated *E*mission of *R*adiation). The concept of the maser, and laser, was first thought out by N. Bloembergen of Harvard University. An operative maser beam was actually constructed by H.D.E. Jcovil, G. Feher, and H. Seidel of the Bell Telephone Laboratories. The amplification referred to in the abbreviated 'a' is produced by the stored up energy in a small crystal. Students of the Atlantis readings, supported by Cayce's son, Edgar Evans Cayce, believe that this crystal is a throwback to the infamous crystal used by the Sons of Belial to supply the continent with power.

Atlantis's technological advances during this period in her history are fantastic, if Cayce's readings are to be believed. Atlantis surpassed even the incredible spurt of scientific development that has characterized our own western civilization for the past fifty years. According to Cayce, the Atlanteans had developed television, atomic energy, and numerous chemical and mechanical processes to aid daily life.

The greatest advancements of Atlantis, however, seem to have been in the field of transportation. At least this field is dealt with most heavily in the readings. Page after page of life readings describe the marvelous way in which people could fly through the air in types of craft. Furthermore, Cayce hinted at a type of travel that went beyond machines, rendering them unnecessary. His suggestion that the Atlanteans could travel through elements other than the air, and could also transmit thoughts through the ether, present innumerable possibilities of outer and inner space communications, as well as inter-dimensional travel.

Did the Atlantean Crystal Power Noah's Ark?

Within the last decade or so, some very fine minds — both in and out of the ecclesiastical establishment — have begun to theorize quite openly about the possibility of the representatives of some advanced technology having interacted with the prophets and revelators of the Bible. Some have written serious works about UFOs and Holy Scriptures. Others have entertained the notion of such activity from church pulpit or classroom lectern.

As an example pertinent to this chapter, some of these speculators have wondered if Noah might not have possessed electricity on board his gigantic ark. The point of discussion has to do with the fact that there are two quite different Hebrew words used to describe what is translated as a "window" or "opening" in the ark.

There is *Challon* or "opening" out of which Noah released the birds that would bring back word of the Great Deluge's having abated. But the first reference, in Genesis 6:16, employs the word *tsohar*, which does not mean either window or opening, but is a Hebrew word so old that most scholars are uncertain of its exact interpretation. According to Jochmans:

> Where it [*tsohar*] is used on twenty-three other occasions in the Old Testament, it is given the meaning, "a brightness, brilliance, the light of the noon-day sun." Its cognates have the word refer to something that glitters or shines." Many Jewish scholars of the traditional school identify the *tsohar* as "a light which has its origin in a shining crystal." Hebrew tradition for centuries has described the *tsohar* as an enormous gem or pearl that Noah hung up from the roof of the Ark, and by power contained within itself lighted the entire vessel for the duration of the Flood voyage.

Atlantean enthusiasts will surely seize upon the above reference to a power source contained within a shining crystal as suggestive of the legendary crystals said to have served as everything from energy plants to destructive weapons for the lost science of Atlantis. Perhaps, such an advocate of Atlantean lore will theorize, the story of the Great Flood is symbolical of the sinking of Atlantis. Noah may have been a surviving Atlantean piloting his mercy ship by means of one of the power crystals.

The Second Destruction

As the laws of nature were made increasingly to bend to the will of man, they almost inevitably began to be used destructively. The struggle of the Children of the Law of One continued unabated against the Sons of Belial. The siege, however, had begun to take on ominous import. As the destructive aspect of physical laws found more and more expression from those of an opportunist nature, and as more and more spiritual laws were manipulated to appease material desires, the louder did the inner earth voice its objections. The days of the Second Destruction were not far off.

There is some indication that a shifting of the poles occurred along with the Second Destruction, though this is not clear. It is interesting to note that Cayce placed the time of the great dinosaurs within this period, and even drew a correlation between the use of the crystal to rid the earth of these beasts and the subsequent unleashing of the upset forces of nature.

The havoc created by this second period of destruction succeeded in breaking up the continent of Atlantis into five major islands, the largest and most advanced of which was Poseidia. A number of people managed to migrate during the months it took to break up the land, while the greater portion of the population stoically awaited their destiny.

As with the First Destruction, a great deal of the dissension between the two ideologically opposed groups arose over the treatment of the "things." By this time these creatures, some of them carrying physical deformities such as feathered appendages, webbed feet, and other animal-like features, were completely enslaved by the Sons of Belial. These selfish souls were unable to see the "things" as people, and had degraded them to a lesser status than that accorded machines.

The Creation of Manimals

As an extra, insidious feature of Atlantean culture, the Sons of Belial soon discovered cybernetic control of the human brain. They cracked the DNA code, enabling them to shape heredity. Such control resting in unethical hands could only result in the creation of more "things."

There are even those who insist that the pig was an Atlantean creation, with man serving as the base material. Proponents of this theory will point out that pork is the meat most similar in substance to human flesh, and the most difficult for man to digest. They will also call attention to the ancient Jewish taboo applied to the ingestion of pork, and remind one of the Greek myth of Circe, the enchantress who turned men into swine.

In Atlantis, such a manipulation of the laws of heredity proved too great a mockery of the Creative Forces, as Cayce always called them. The fatal strain of *hubris* had to be weeded out. The Sons of Belial had become such an effrontery to nature that it was these forces, in the end, that destroyed them.

As with the First and Second Destructions, the final demise of Atlantis did not happen catastrophically, nor was it without warning. The volcanic eruptions and the breaking up of the land occurred over several months, each tremor increasingly more damaging. These signs, as well as other psychic impressions were heeded by the Children of the Law of One. Several of them migrated to the Pyrenees, Egypt, the Yucatan, and Og, or what is now Peru.

Preserving the Atlantean Records

The imminence of the coming disaster prompted feverish activity among recordkeepers. The readings are quite emphatic on this point. Repeatedly a client was told by Cayce that he had been connected with the preserving of the records, and that his work of that lifetime would soon be discovered in modern times.

There were three principal caches of Atlantean historical records. One set of records was allegedly left in a temple in the Yucatan, which can still be seen; one set resides in the Hall of Records, a small pyramid in Egypt as yet undiscovered—publicly, at least—but which is prophesied to be found before the end of the century; and the third set sunk with Atlantis.

This third set of records, however, was reportedly contained in the Poseidian temple of Iltar, and this temple is to rise intact, the records preserved.

It was the rising of this temple that Cayce indicated would herald the eventual complete re-emergence of Atlantis. There is recent archaeological evidence in support of such an occurrence, offered by the discovery of an ancient sunken "temple" off the coast of Bimini, in the Caribbean Sea. It was in this area that Cayce had placed the temple of Iltar.

But the temple was still above water when the warnings were received and the records placed in it. These records are supposed to detail man's spiritual and physical history upon the earth. A goodly portion covers the history of Atlantis, as that was where the metamorphosis from spirit to flesh had occurred.

The greatest percentage of Cayce's Atlantean readings reflect life during, and immediately preceding, this third and final destruction. Much of the information for this period of time is gleaned from the voluminous Egyptian readings, for Egypt was the colony to which the majority of Atlanteans fled.

Healing in the Temple Beautiful

One of the most significant things achieved by the Atlanteans before their assimilation into Egyptian culture was the payment of their ages-old debt to the grossly misused "things." In the readings detailing the correction of their physical deformities, Cayce gave a number of exciting insights into the art of healing.

Many undersea divers, including scientists and U.S. Army officers, have spotted the remains of city walls, roadways, dams, and buildings off Florida.

This healing took place in two temples, called the Temple of Sacrifice and the Temple Beautiful. In the first temple physical corrections were made; in the latter, the Soul was purified, and creative abilities were developed.

In the Temple of Sacrifice the feathered appendages and other animal features were removed. The Atlanteans had discovered the healing properties of color and music, and these were heavily employed. Massage was also used, for the Atlanteans believed that physical manipulation would raise the subject's own healing powers to his highest spiritual center, whence this power would spill over into the entire body and promote healing. Undesignated "electrical forces" were used in an unspecified manner to remove unnatural appendages, either surgically, one presumes, or perhaps through dematerialization.

The Children of the Law of One did not terminate their obligations to the "things" with the simple rendering of physical perfection. As spiritual beings, they knew that their true purpose was to fan the fire of the divine spark dwelling within these Souls. For, as some enthusiasts of genetically produced physical perfection forget, a beautiful body does not necessarily insure a beautiful personality. The Atlans, as Cayce called them, realized this; and in the Temple Beautiful, a Soul was awakened to its spiritual heritage, then trained in the arts, which the Atlans believed serve man as reminders not to stray from the positive path.

Is America the Reincarnation of Atlantis?

Edgar Cayce tells us that the vast majority of the American populace has experienced past lives on the continent of Atlantis. If Cayce could go as far as to state that America is largely populated by former Atlanteans, then it would seem only a short step to declaring that America herself is the reincarnation of Atlantis. In the United States, we have been given an opportunity to develop our civilization to the point of the same crucial decision encountered by the Atlanteans: power for the good of Earth and her people, or power for evil.

The Law of cause and effect may seem unnecessarily harsh to some, but to those who trust it, it is the law of compassion. According to the precepts of reincarnation and Karma, if a man — or a nation — errs and strays from the path, he is not condemned for all eternity. All is not staked on one throw of the dice.

If such is the case, and America truly is Atlantis reincarnated, then it is evident that we are fast approaching that crucial hour of decision. All the necessary cards have been dealt: we have split the atom; we have confused the natural evolution of our planet with pollutants; we have cracked the DNA code and can duplicate it in our laboratories; we have developed weapons of destruction so powerful that one thimble-full of bacteria can destroy all life forms on Earth; and anti-ballistic missile silos —with government support — are defacing the landscape.

We are truly being confronted by the other side of the two-faced results of technological advances. The one side promises knowledge gained to aid mankind, to end disease, to increase crops, to promote production of labor-saving devices. The other side leers at the destructiveness made possible by the same knowledge.

The final choice made by Atlantis, even in allegory, if not reality, is overwhelmingly evident by its totally complete destruction. The choice we as citizens of the United States of America will have to make may one day make itself known by the same cataclysmic changes.

Cayce's entranced delineation of a nation dying at the hand of its own perverted super science seem to contain definite foreshadowings and forewarnings of our own struggle with a technology that bends and twists moral considerations. Indeed, Cayce may not have been reading the past records of Atlantis at all: he may have received a vision of the future of the United States.

IV

Prehistoric Scientists And Hero-Gods

It is the consensus of orthodox scientists that although the earth may be billions of years old, human civilization has existed for but a few thousand years. The majority of historians and archaeologists state that man's history of civilization is coincident with man's own written records. Anything that occurred before man, as we know him, learned to write his journals, diaries, and accounts is "pre-history." History, then, is generally accepted as encompassing about 6,000 years, a startlingly infinitesimal 1/5000 of one percent of the estimated age of Earth.

Although many readers may deem Edgar Cayce's mystic vision of an Atlantis sinking into the ocean due to the moral erosion of an unprincipled super science as a bit too fantastic for easy palatability, a serious and determined handful of archaeologists, the great majority of them persistent amateurs, believe that pre-historic civilizations—call them Atlantis, Lemuria, and Mu, or whatever you please—have attained high levels of technology before succumbing to natural or man-made cataclysms. These civilizations may not have attained the levels of scientific accomplishment envisioned by Cayce, but enough evidence is being steadily uncovered that indicates that "historic man" has but relearned a great deal from "pre-historic man."

Ancient Egyptian Schoolchildren
Knew Earth Is Round

Dr. Samuel A. B. Mercer, professor emeritus of Semitic and Egyptian languages at Trinity College, University of Toronto, spent over six years completing translations of the hieroglyphs carved into five small pyramids near Sakkara, Egypt. In 1953, Dr. Mercer published a four-volume work of the translations, a task which had been originally initiated by a series of Egyptologists soon after the hieroglyphs were discovered in 1880.

The hieroglyphs, considered to be the oldest written records of mankind, reveal that Egyptian children were taught that the world was round more than 3,600 years before Columbus set sail under the aegis of the Spanish crown to prove the same fact to a doubting Europe. Egyptian students were given a curriculum of history, astronomy, medicine, engineering, agriculture, and the household arts.

They were also tutored in a highly developed legal system and a moral and religious philosophy. Since we have already noted the strange cultural fact that Egyptian civilizations virtually began at its peak and worked its way downward, the question comes at once to mind: who taught the ancient Egyptians an academic curriculum that could not have been equalled in fifteenth century Europe?

The Mystery Woman In the Mountain of Fire

During the 1952-53 Thirstland Expedition to southern and central Africa's desert zones, explorer-leader John Brown sent back an account of a remarkable specimen of cave art found in the Mountains of Fire. According to Brown, the main paintings, located in a dark cave, were quite unlike any of the usual Bushman work. The central figure was a pretty white woman, young, graceful, with her hair bobbed in the style of Ancient Egypt. She wore a beaded head-dress, a garment that resembled a modern jersey blouse, shorts, gloves, girdle, and shoes similar to those worn in modern Mediterranean countries.

A natural rock amphitheater nearby appears to have been used in ancient times. Could Brown and the Thirstland Expedition have found evidence of a visiting Atlantean priestess or aristocrat, a lovely prehistory woman who dressed in a manner that would cause no heads to turn unduly if she were to walk down a street in Chicago?

But how strange her garments must have appeared to the ancient African artisans who captured her image in stone. How like a goddess she must have seemed. She may even have spoken or sung in the natural amphitheater under the illumination of electric lights.

Dry Cell Batteries from 250 B.C.

In 1938, while digging in a hill near Baghdad, German archaeologist Wilhelm Konig turned up an object that resembled a modern day dry cell battery. A bit later he learned that four similar objects had been found a few miles downriver. In a museum in Berlin, Konig discovered ten additional dry cells exactly like the one he had unearthed in his original digging. The batteries in the museum, however, had been broken down into their component parts.

Willard F. B. Gray of the General Electric High Voltage Laboratory in Pittsfield, Massachusetts, built a duplicate of the ancient battery using the dimensions and metallurgical analysis supplied him by German scientist-author Willy Ley. Gray used copper sulphate instead of an electrolyte which, of course, was unknown to the archaeologists, and the battery worked perfectly.

It has been assumed by some researchers that the Parthians, who once inhabited the area in which Konig discovered the battery, may have used the current from the batteries for electroplating metal, circa 250 B.C. Most archaeologists who have given the matter any attention doubt that the Parthians invented the battery, but, rather, were bequeathed the secret by the ancient Babylonians or Sumerians. But then, by all previously cherished archaeological tenets, those ancient peoples were certainly not to have possessed such utilitarian items as dry cell batteries any more than the Parthians.

Again we are left with the enigma of whether our ancestors at the dawn of history were as scientifically sophisticated as our progenitors of little more than 200 years ago (Volta is given credit for inventing the dry cell battery in the early 1800s), or whether the ancients were, for a time, able to maintain certain items of technology given to them by the survivors of an advanced prehistoric civilization. Either concept violates our long cherished image of the sandal and toga, sword and bow peoples of 250 B.C.

Electric Batteries in 2000 B.C.

Other batteries have since been located. In some sites, groups of clay pots have been found together with thin iron and copper rods, which may have been used to connect the pots into a series so that stronger voltage might be produced.

The vast majority of the ancient batteries that have been located date from the Parthian period of Persian occupation of the region, between 250 B.C. and 650 A.D. But electroplated objects — or so they certainly appear — have been discovered in Babylonian ruins that date back to 2000 B.C.

Auguste Mariette, a famous nineteenth-century French archaeologist, unearthed a number of electroplated artifacts at a depth of 60 feet in the area of the Sphinx of Giza. In the *Grand Dictionaire Universal du*^{ieme} *Siècle*, Mariette described the artifacts as being "pieces of gold jewelry whose thinness and lightness makes one believe they had been produced by electroplating, an industrial technique that we have been using only two or three years."

Joey R. Jochmans is among those who have speculated that since the ancient Egyptians possessed electricity to electroplate gold jewelry, they might also have utilized it to illuminate the intricately devised passageways in their tombs.

Jochmans points out that the traditionally accepted means of illumination available to the Egyptians would limit their lighting to torches and oil lamps, but no trace of smoke or soot has been found on the ceilings of the pyramids or the subterranean tombs of the Pharaohs in the Valley of the Kings

"It has been thought that perhaps the Egyptians used some complicated system of lenses and mirrors to bring sunlight into the burial chambers," Jochmans says, "but no remains of any such system have ever been found. There are a number of ancient tombs with tunnels and passageways that are too complex for a mirror system to have brought sufficient light into the inner chamber. The only other alternative is that the Egyptians had a smokeless light source."

But could that "smokeless light source" really have been electricity?

Did The Ancient Egyptians Have Television?

Some theorists, Jochmans among them, have even suggested that the wall engravings in the Temple of Dendere, built during the Ptolemaic period, depict men handling what could be Crookes tubes, the forerunner of the modern television tube. Jochmans writes:

> When the [Crookes] tube is in operation, the ray originates where the cathode electrical wire enters the tube, and from here the ray extends through the length of the tube to the opposite end. In the temple picture, the electron beam is represented as an outstretched serpent. The tail of the serpent begins where a cable from the energy box enters the tube, and the serpent's head touches the opposite end. In Egyptian art, the serpent was the symbol of divine energy.
>
> . . . The Temple picture shows one tube, on the extreme left of the picture, to be operating under normal conditions. But with the second tube, situated closest to the energy box on the right, an interesting experiment has been portrayed. Michael R. Freedman, an electric and electromagnetic engineer, believes that the solar disc

on Horus' head is a Van de Graaff generator, an apparatus which collects static electricity. A baboon is portrayed holding a metal knife between Van de Graaff-solar disc and the second tube. Under actual conditions, the static charge built up on the knife from the generator would cause the electron beam inside the Crookes tube to be diverted from the normal path, because the negative knife and negative beam would repel each other. In the Temple picture, the serpent's head in the second tube is turned away from the end of the tube, repulsed by the knife in the baboon's hand.

Such theorists as Jochmans are convinced that every aspect of the Temple picture represents an important feature of a "serious scientific experiment."

Egypt: Heir of Atlantis

With the artifacts that continue to be unearthed at important dig sites around the world, one cannot state with any pronounced degree of certainty that the ancient Egyptians were not in possession of electron tubes. But it seems rather likely that if they were manipulating such electronic objects, they may have "inherited" them from a culture superior to their own.

And, of course, that suggestion provokes the controversy about "ancient astronauts" from some extraterrestrial source and revives the much older conflict concerning superscientists from a lost continent, such as Atlantis. Indeed, if one speculates about "worlds before our own," then one must be prepared to be open to either hypothesis.

At this moment in time and space there may not be enough dramatic evidence to convince the academics that either hypothesis is a tenable one — that any spacecraft from another planet landed here to take possession of our liquid green planet or that a mighty nation sank under the Atlantic Ocean — but the evidence seems to be steadily accumulating that civilization has been cyclical upon this terrestrial globe and that as rabbinical literature states, "worlds upon worlds there were before Adam was."

In regard to the ancient Egyptian electron tubes, electromagnetics engineer Professor S. R. Harris identified a box-and-braided cable in the picture as "virtually an exact copy of engineering illustrations used today for representing a bundle of conducting electrical wires." The cable runs from the box the full length of the floor and terminates at both the ends and at the bases of two peculiar objects resting on two pillars. Professor Harris is said to have identified these representations as high voltage insulators.

X-Ray Machines From 500 B.C.

When German scientist Wilhelm Roentgen accidentally discovered the X-ray in 1895, medical science knew that it now possessed a means by which thousands of lives could be prolonged and years of suffering might be avoided. But current evidence exists that both the ancient Chinese and Indians had operable X-ray machines over 2,500 years ago.

Jivaka, a contemporary of the Guatama Buddha, taught that it was essential to illuminate the organs of the body before making a diagnosis or performing surgical operations. Jivaka, whoever he may really have been, practiced trepanning and other surgical techniques so sophisticated in comparison with his contemporaries that his skill has become incorporated in several legends. The "King of Doctors," as Jivaka was called, possessed a "gem" that when set before a patient, "illuminated his body as a lamp lights up all the objects in a house, and so revealed the nature of his malady."

The Chinese Emperor Kao-tsu, founder of the Han Dynasty in 206 B.C., discovered the "precious mirror that illuminates the bones of the body" in the palace of Emperor Ch'in-chi, the last ruler of the Chin Dynasty, his immediate predecessor. Again, we can only wonder if such a marvelous artifact was but a remnant of a great prehistoric civilization, a remnant somehow kept functional by carefully trained "keepers of the secret."

The "mirror" has been described as having been rectangular, four feet wide by five feet and nine inches high, brilliant on both its outer and inner sides. When an invalid stood before the "mirror," his image appeared reversed. With his hands placed over his heart, the five viscera could be observed unobstructed by any obstacle. Hidden maladies of troubled patients could be found by placing them in front of the remarkable illuminating mirror.

Since mankind had to do without widespread utilization of an X-ray machine until Roentgen's discovery, or rediscovery in 1895, it would seem that neither the ancient Indians nor Chinese actually invented the magical "gem" or "mirror," but that some advanced prehistoric civilization bequeathed them both machines and knowledge that the ancients were simply not yet technologically sophisticated enough to perpetuate.

Think About It This Way . . .

We might consider the analogy of our own twentieth-century medical missionaries who work among primitive peoples. Let us hypothesize the unpleasant situation of the entire civilized world blowing itself to nuclear bits in an insane orgy of violence.

Although their world has been destroyed, the medical missionaries continue to work among the primitive peoples, who are only dimly aware that a terrible man-made cataclysm has occurred in their benefactors' homelands. After a time, the medical missionaries grow old and do their best to instruct the more intelligent of the natives in the ways of medicine—how to take a blood count, how to remove an appendix, how to operate the X-ray machines.

When the medical missionaries die, the native physicians take over the jungle hospitals. By now, most of the medical supplies from the destroyed nations have been supplanted by native herbs. In some cases, primitive remedies are prescribed after the malady has been diagnosed by the still operable X-ray machine.

PURSUIT *Newsletter.*

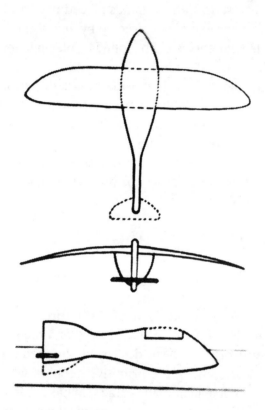

Dr. Khalil Messiha believes that he has found evidence to indicate that the Egyptians had flying machines as early as the third or fourth century B.C. Dr. Messiha discovered a model glider or airplane when he was looking through a box of bird models in one of the Cairo Museum's storerooms. Dr. Messiha's brother, a flight engineer, agrees with him that the model, made of sycamore wood, bears a striking resemblance to the American Hercules transport plane.

Then, one day, the generators break down, and there is no one who remembers how to repair them. And even if there were, there is no longer Los Angeles from which to order parts.

The X-ray machine, the radios, the long-dead dry cell batteries, although still revered, are now useless. They are forgotten, as the natives' survival instinct sends them back into the jungle and into magic in order to practice primitive, but often effective, healing arts. Someday, perhaps two thousand years in the future, someone will "remember" how to use the marvelous machines.

How many desperately imparted lessons did our ancestors forget? Is it so heretical to visualize survivors from a dying civilization seeking by rote and god-like threats to teach the more intelligent of the Egyptians, the Greeks, the Mayas, the Incas how to service and maintain the mechanical objects of their advanced technology?

Ancient Egyptian Airplanes

Dr. Khalil Messiha believes that he has found evidence to indicate that the Egyptians had flying machines as early as the third or fourth century B.C. What is more, Dr. Messiha's brother, a flight engineer, agrees with him and adds that the aerofoil shape of the models discovered among some ancient bird figures demonstrates a "drag effect" evolved only recently after many years of aeronautical engineering research.

Dr. Messiha found the model glider or airplane in 1969 when he was looking through a box of bird models in one of the Cairo Museum's storerooms. The glider, made of sycamore wood, bears a striking resemblance, Dr. Messiha has since learned, to the American Hercules transport plane, which has a distinctive wing shape.

Most of the bird figures that have been found at excavations in Egypt are half-human, half-bird in design, but this object was very different. It seemed to be a model of a high-winged monoplane with a heart-shaped fuselage, which assumes a compressed ellipse toward the tail.

"It is the tail that is really the most interesting thing which distinguishes this model from all other that have been discovered," Dr. Messiha was quoted in the May 18, 1972, issue of the *London Times*. The tail, it seems, has a vertical fin. There is no known bird that flies equipped with a rudder.

"No bird can produce such a contortion at the rear of its body to assume anything that looks like the model. Furthermore there is a groove under the fin for a tailplane [cross-piece] which is missing," the *Times* added.

In addition, Dr. Messiha had learned from his several-year study of Egyptian bird figures, all other models had been lavishly decorated and had been fitted for legs. The glider has no legs and only very slight traces of an eye that had been painted on one side of the "nose," together with two faint reddish lines under the wing.

Dr. Messiha pointed out for Michael Frenchman of the *Times* that the ancient Egyptian engineers always made models of contemporary things, from their funeral boats to their war chariots.

We know that funeral boats and chariots existed, because their full-scale versions have been found in addition to their models. Dr. Messiha has come to believe that the glider that he discovered in a box of relics excavated at Saqqara in 1898 is a scale model of a full-sized flying machine of some kind.

According to the *Times*, Dr. Messiha studied fine art for five years before he took up medicine. The 48-year-old doctor is also an illustrator and an engraver, and some years ago he received a prize for constructing model aircraft. "This glider is very much like some of the scale model planes I used to make 20 years ago," he said.

"This is no toy model," Dr. Messiha emphasized. "It is too scientifically designed and it took a lot of skill to make it."

The doctor is presently engaged in research in ancient Egyptian sciences and engineering. Dr. Messiha believes that the Egyptians were very advanced in certain areas of technology, "including elementary aeronautics."

INFO Journal, Spring, 1973, found it "significant" that the glider had come to the Cairo Museum from the dig at Saqqara:

> At Saqqara about 2700 B.C. the first Egyptian pyramid was built for the second king of the Third Dynasty, Netekhet (or Zoser, as the Greeks would later call him). Zoser's architect was credited by the later Egyptians as having invented the art of building in hewn stone, as being a great astronomer, magician, and the father of medicine. He came to be deified as the son of the god Ptah, and the Greeks long afterward identified him with Asklepios, their own god of medicine.
>
> Saqqara was a shrine for millenia .... The little airplane could have been the brainchild of Imhotep, dreaming of flight, or of some other practical dreamer such as Archytas of Tarentum. Archytas (c. 400 B.C.) ... is also alleged to have devised a flying machine in the form of a dove, propelled by compressed air. ...

A. Neuburger's *Technical Arts and Sciences of the Ancients* agrees: "Archytas of Tarentum, about 400-365 B.C., set in motion a flying machine in the form of a wooden dove by means of compressed air." Archytas was a Greek philosopher and a friend of Plato.

The Limitless Expanse of Prehistoric Genius

Somehow we nod our heads in understanding and in respect for the genius of the early people of the Mediterranean coastlines. After all, the seeds of Western civilization and culture, which culminated in the magnificence that is our very selves, were sown in that area. Even we laymen become somewhat uncomfortable when we learn about such sites as Ben Chiang in Thailand, because we are forced to deal with the reality that there appear to have been several very ancient "cradles of civilization."

In 1968, Dr. Korium Megertchian, a Soviet archaeologist, unearthed the oldest large-scale metallurgical factory in the world at Medzamor in Russian Armenia.

Incredible as it may seem, at this site, 4,500 years ago, an unknown prehistoric people worked more than 200 furnaces in order to produce an assortment of vases, knives, spearheads, rings, bracelets, and other metal items. Safety-conscious, the prehistoric craftsmen of Medzamor wore mouth-filters and gloves while they worked. Evidence present at the site indicated that they made their wares of copper, lead, zinc, iron, gold, tin, manganese, and as many as fourteen varieties of bronze.

The productive smelters also produced an assortment of metallic paints, ceramics, and glass, but as the scientists admitted freely, the most anachronistic item was several pairs of tweezers, fashioned of steel and unearthed from layers dating back before the first millenium B.C. Metallurgical experts in the Soviet Union, the United States, Britain, France, and Germany later verified the claim that the steel used in the tweezers was of an excelptionally high grade.

Reporting in *Science et Vie*, July, 1969, French journalist Jean Vidal stated his belief that such finds as those at Medzamor indicate an unknown period of technological development.

In Vidal's opinion: "Medzamor was founded by wise men of earlier civilizations. They possessed knowledge they had acquired during a remote age unknown to us, that deserved to be called scientific and industrial."

In his privately published manuscript, *The Legacy of Methuselah*, Joey Jochmans makes the observation that what makes the Medzamor metallurgical site especially interesting to those in the Judeo-Christian tradition is that "it is within fifteen miles of Mount Ararat — the landing site of the survivors [Noah and his family] of the destroyed Antediluvian civilization."

According to what we know of aluminum, it was not discovered until 1807 and it was not produced successfully in pure form until 1957. Even today the process of extracting aluminum from bauxite mineral is a very complicated process, which involves the utilization of a Reverbier oven, a refraction chamber and regenerator, as well as electrolysis and the production of temperatures which must exceed 1,000 degrees centigrade.

With that bit of technical trivia out of the way, we may now deal with the puzzling discovery that was made in China at the burial site of Chou Chu, a general of the Tsin era, who lived about 265 to 316 A.D. The astonishing artifact in this case was a belt fastener that was not only made of metal with openwork ornamentation, but was composed of an alloy of 5 percent manganese, 10 percent copper and *85 percent aluminum.*

Although orthodox researchers are not able to concede that the exquisite glass miniatures produced by Egyptian craftsmen as early as 3000 B.C. are "among the most astounding achievements in the history of glassmaking," they believe that "industrial chemistry in antiquity, though tremendously impressive, was strictly a trial-and-error affair."

Writing in the September, 1964 issue of *National Geographic*, Ray Winfield Smith states: "The ancients of the Mediterranean and the East were intelligent and practical people. Yet when I speak of cerium and lanthanum, of antimony and manganese, of lead oxides, soad, and lime, you must not think that the artisans of those times understood the chemistry of these ingredients as we do. . . . Glass-makers simply knew that certain substances in nature—in rock, sand, earth, or ashes—gave special properties to their products. . . . "

If glassmaking was such a hit-and-miss, trial-and-error procedure, we must certainly wonder how such a massive piece of glass as that found in a cave near Haifa, Israel in 1966 ever came into being. Although this area has been a famous glass-making region since the time of the Phoenicians, this slab of glass is eleven feet long, seven feet wise, 1 1/2 feet thick, and weights 8.8 tons. The piece of glass is a solid one, raspberry-colored with greenish streaks.

Sanskrit Accounts of Indian Aircraft

While Dr. Messiha credited the ancient Egyptians with "elementary" aeronautical knowledge, G.R. Josyer, director of the International Academy of Sanskrit Research in Mysore, India, stated on September 25, 1952, that Indian manuscripts several thousands of years old dealt with the construction of various types of aircraft for civil aviation and for warfare.

The specific manuscript on aeronautics included plans of three types of *vimanas* (aircraft), the *Rukna, Sundara,* and *Shakuna*. Five hundred stanzas of an ancient text treat of such intricate details as the choice and preparation of metals which would be suitable for various parts of *vimanas* of different types.

Although the ancient manuscripts had been compiled by venerable scribes and priests, the stanzas did not discuss the mysticism of the Hindu philosophy of Atman or Brahman, but detailed more mundane matters that the learned men of old had considered essential for the "existence of man and the progress of nations both in time of peace and war." These vital bits of information, according to Mr Josyer, included the design of a helicopter-type cargo plane, specially constructed to carry combustibles and ammunition, and the drawings for double-and triple-decked passenger planes, capable of transporting as many as 500 persons.

There were eight chapters in the aeronautics manuscript that provided plans for the construction of aircraft that flew in the air, traveled under water, for floated pontoon-like on the water's surface. Some stanzas told of the qualifications and training of pilots. The ancient *vimanas* were equipped with cameras radio, and a kind of radar system.

When word of the Sanskrit manuscripts reached beyond the monasteries in which they had been kept, the academy in Mysore began to receive a great deal of worldwide pressure to translate the ancient texts. Thus, at the age of eighty-one, Mr. Josyer "had to sit up and translate the technical Sanskrit into readable English, and scrutinize the printing of both the Sanskrit and the English.

The aged scholar found that the *Vymankia Shastra* consisted of "nearly 6,000 lines, or 3,000 verses of lucid Sanskrit dealing with the constructions of airplanes. That the vocabulary of ancient Sanskrit could in simple flowing verse depict the technical details with effortless ease in a tribute to the language — and the greatness of the author." (The work is attributed to Maharshi Bharadwaja, a Hindu sage who recorded the spiritual, intellectual, and scientific fields of ancient Indian civilization.)

The translation was finally published in book form by the Coronation Press of Mysore in 1973. In his foreword to the work, Mr. Josyer presents his assessment of the implications of the *Vymankia Shastra*:

> The 20th Century may be said to be made historic by two achievements: The bringing of Moon-rock from outer space and the publication of *Vymankia Shastra* from the unknown past. . . The *Vymankia Shastra* is a cornucopia of previous formulas for the manufacture of aeroplanes, which should make Lindberg, Rolls, Zeppelin, DeHavilland, Tupolev, and Harold Gray of Pan American, gape in astonishment, and if duly worked up, herald a new era of Aeroplane manufacture of the benefit of the benefit of Mankind.

Ancient scientists insisted that any who would seek to pilot a *vimana* should acquaint himself thoroughly with 32 secrets of the working of the craft. As one examines the "secrets," he finds a peculiar mixture of technology and mysticism, almost as if pilot and craft achieve a kind of harmony and unit as one single, living entity. One should, for example, learn such techniques as the following in order to pilot a *vimana*:

Maantrika: The invoking of mantras which will permit one to achieve certain spiritual and hypnotic powers so that he can construct aeroplanes which cannot be destroyed.

Taantrika: By acquiring some of the tantric powers, one may endow his aircraft with those same powers.

Goodha: This secret permits the pilot to make his *vimana* invisible to his enemies. *Adrishya* accomplishes the same purpose by attracting "the force of the ethereal flow in the sky."

Paroksha: This helpful hint enables the pilot to paralyze other *vimanas* and put them out of action.

Aparoksha: One may employ this ability to project a beam of light in front of his craft to light his way.

Viroopa Karana: With this skill mastered, the pilot can produce "the thirty-second kind of smoke," charge it with "the light of the heat waves in the sky" and transform his craft into a "very fierce and terrifying shape," guaranteed to cause "utmost fright to onlookers." *Roopaanara* can cause the *vimana* to assume such shapes as those of the lion, tiger, rhinoceros, serpent — even a mountain — to confuse observers.

Suroopa: If one can attract the thirteen kinds of "Karaka force," one can make the *vimana* appear to be a "heavenly damsel bedecked with flowers and jewels."

An Expedition In Search of Atlantis

In July, 1973, a group composed of educators, students, scientists, parapsychologists, and psychics embarked on a six-week expedition in search of Atlantis off Cadiz, Spain. Leading the expedition was Maxine Asher (who at that time served as educational consultant to Pepperdine University in California and who is still head of the Ancient Mediterranean Research Association) and her coodirector, Dr. Julian Nava, vice-chairman of the Los Angeles City Board of Education and a professor of history at California State University, Northridge.

When I interviewed the attractive, enthusiastic Ms. Asher shortly before her early departure for Spain, she informed me that Dr. Manson Valentine, Gail Cayce (granddaughter of the famous clairvoyant), and Edgerton Sykes, a noted Atlantean scholar, would be accompanying her party. In addition, she said, they had been

Ever in search of evidence of Atlantean survival sites, Dr. Maxine Asher climbs ancient ruins near Corinth, Greece.

promised assistance from the Scripps Institute of Oceanography in San Diego and cooperation from the Spanish Ministry of Education and Science. In that same spirit of cooperation, Ms. Asher patiently answered my questions while she attended to a multitude of last-minute details.

Your expedition is seeking Atlantis off the coast of Spain. What do you believe the perimeters of the continent to have been?

Maxine Asher: I believe they extended as far south as the Canary Islands, on the back side of the Atlantic, and as far north as Ireland. I can't say *where* in Ireland, but I suspect as far as Galway, County Cork, and maybe a little farther. I think that Atlantis spanned the entire Atlantic Ocean at one time, perhaps one million or two million or more years ago; it's hard to date it at this point.

I believe that its northernmost boundaries on the other side were perhaps Nova Scotia, and the southernmost boundaries, Bimini, and maybe farther down. I know that everyone is saying, Yucatan, Peru; but I'm really not sure that it went too much farther than, say, Venezuela. Surely, its people could have migrated, but I don't see its perimeters extending that far.

Atlantis probably went down originally as a result of seismic upheavals under the ocean, but I do believe the final destruction was probably cosmically ordained. Hypothesizing, of course, the final destruction of Atlantis could have come cosmically, because the people had become so evil and had generated enough negative force that they had disrupted the Cosmos. Divine Retribution could have been the spring-board—let me call it that—for the cosmic upheaval that destroyed Atlantis.

What level of civilization would you say the Atlanteans had attained?

Ms. Asher: Well, I think that's like asking what were the Americans like. We need to look at the Colonial Period and the Civil War. I would say that, technologically, around 50,000 B.C., they were very, very advanced. The had air travel, and they had underwater devices. They were very "modern."

Comparable to our contemporary civilization?

Ms. Asher: Comparable, but I don't think they were beyond. I don't think you can reconstruct Atlantis and find another United States, however. I think it probably was a different type of culture.

It is difficult to evaluate just what "advanced" is. When the pioneers traveled across the early United States, they said the Indians were in a less advanced state of civilization — but by whose standards?

The Atlanteans, I believe, did have a highly advanced technology; but I believe their technology was psychically oriented. They combined the psychic and the rational in such a molding that they were able to do some very impossible things, such as moving huge rocks for pyramids through psychokinesis. They read each other telepathically. In its most advanced period, life was probably very much governed by a combination of the best of two worlds — and they lived in harmony. I think we need now to look at what happened to them because, according to many accounts, they faced a decline that probably came about as a result of forces that were negative.

Do you believe they have had nuclear power?

Ms. Asher: I believe they had a form of energy as powerful as our nuclear energy, but I believe that it was psychic in nature.

I don't have to tell you, Brad, about the force of the psychic. If enough people get together for bad, using mind control, they can do an awful lot of damage.

Why are you led to Cadiz? Why not Nova Scotia?

Ms. Asher: Well, first of all, when I was doing my Masters' work in history, I spent much time trying to find the origin of the Etruscans. [Ms. Asher has, since this interview, received her doctorate.] I went to the Etruscan tombs and so forth, and nothing made any sense.

So I went to Crete, and there I became bothered by the origin of Linear A. writing.

I scooted up to the Pyrenees Mountains, and I got bugged to death about Cro-Magnon man.

I began to tear around, looking for common origins, not even thinking of Atlantis.

I was led, I am sure, by the Divine Hand to Spain.

When I got to Cadiz—Plato had spoken about Atlantis lying beyond the Gates of Hercules—the vibrations were so strong, Brad, I thought I was going to jump out of my skin.

The first person I met was a taxi driver, who went into an entire dissertation on Atlantis. One thing led to another. I interviewed many people, and I said, "By God, I think Plato knew what he was talking about!"

I did extensive research on Cadiz, and I went to the university and they accepted my program. Not so much on Atlantis, but on the search for it. All knowledge, they stated, is transient; all knowledge is changing; and the finding of Atlantis will only be a vehicle, a doorway, that will open up a whole brave New World for many of us.

I think Cadiz is a logical place to begin, but I suspect that we will be uncovering pieces of Atlantis all the way from Cadiz to Ireland. I'll be doing research in the Erin Islands in Ireland shortly because the Irish connection may, in fact, be more important than the Spanish, although all of it will be meaningful.

Do you feel any currently existing lands were once a part of Atlantis?

Ms. Asher: I think part of the Iberian peninsula was, specifically the area near the Guandalquiver River. I think that area could have been Tartessos and that there could have been a land bridge of sorts connecting that point to the Atlantean island.

I think Edgar Cayce was mistaken—again, I am hypothesizing—when he said that Poseidia was near Bimini. He said that the Atlanteans buried some of their records in the Pyrenees Mountains, in Egypt, and also in Yucatan; but I still suspect that Poseidia, bearing the name of the Greek god of the sea, was the last little island near Cadiz, and that the Atlanteans brought their records to the obvious place close at hand.

Do you believe that Atlantis is the true name of the lost continent?

Ms. Asher: I don't know, but I believe that it had the combination of letters *Ata* or *Atla* in it.

Those combinations are found often in Central and South America. Do you think that we are the descendants of Atlantean survivors?

Ms. Asher: Yes, but other than the one boat with Noah and the animals, or whatever. I think that there may have been twelve boats, corresponding to the twelve tribes of Israel.

And couldn't there have been Atlantean colonies in other lands?

Ms. Asher: Of course. And I think some people began to leave early. I believe that people began to see the beginning of the end, you know, and took off.

But you also remember that in the biblical story, only a few people believed Noah when he said that there was any sort of danger. That's why we have such isolated pockets of Atlanteans. We have the Basques in Portugal, the Gaelic Irish, and others.

Do you think that we could suffer such a cataclysm in our time?

Ms. Asher: Yes, but it may not be physical. It may be that the world will face some sort of catastrophe that will be psychic in nature and only those who have learned to tap all levels of consciousness will survive.

The expedition of the Ancient Mediterranean Research Associated terminated their search for Atlantis in mid-July, 1973, under a dark cloud filled with confusing rumblings. Reports were issued that Dr. Julian Nava had resigned in disgust because the Cadiz-based team had "blown it" with a premature dive and an exaggerated appraisal of the worth of the find.

Dr. Nava was quoted as saying that on the night of July 16th, just a few days before the extremely hard-to-obtain Spanish Land Permit was to be awarded to AMRA, an authorized dive had been made. When divers released a claim of the "greatest discovery in world history," the disgruntled Spanish government had denied the permit.

Later, Dr. Nava clarified his position that he had resigned as codirector of AMRA only because of the necessity of his returning to the United States in order to meet publishers' deadlines on some textbooks he was writing.

The expedition had began to take on overtones of a James Bond thriller, complete with shadings of international intrigue. (Ms. Asher did, in fact, write a book about the "Atlantean Conspiracy.") Ms. Asher left Spain with a group of students for the comparative quiet of Ireland.

Then, in September, 1973, reports from Cadiz indicated that several Spanish archaeological groups were searching for the site of the Atlantis "find" claimed by the Ancient Mediterranean Research Association on July 16th. AMRA Director Maxine Asher stated that her group was barred from using its official underwater archaeological permits and could not release its photographs or maps of the site until politics in Spain had stabilized.

"It is unfortunate," stated Dr. Asher, "that the scientific and educational interests of the entire world in the matter of Atlantis are thwarted by international intrigue."

An interview in the newspaper *Diario de Cadiz* on September 2, 1973, quoted archaeologist Jesus Aguero as saying, "One thing we cannot doubt is that the city of Atlantis exists . . . we even have Atlantean money, which can be found in the Louvre in Paris."

Professor Aguero further validated that vestiges of Atlantis can be found in the coastal waters north of Gibraltar, the area were the AMRA group first made its finds.

Atlantis in North America

Perhaps those who search for the lost Atlantis would do best to concentrate *inland* on the North American continent, rather than plumbing the depths of the Atlantic Ocean.

A nation can "sink" in many ways. It can lose several degrees of the magnitude it might once have possessed. It can degrade itself by sinking into moral morass. It can destroy itself by internal warfare, political strife, or technologically provoked cataclysm.

One need not claim that the fabled Atlantis existed on North American shores, but there is an astonishing amount of evidence that a number of forgotten people and cultures did flourish in what is now the United States. Those scientists who somehow still cling to a kind of orderly evolutionary progression of Mongolian types transforming themselves into characteristic Amerindian types have got to be ignoring a great many discoveries of diverse and apparently anomalous genetic strains of *Homo sapiens* which once thrived on the North American land mass.

A Garden of Eden for the Giants of Death Valley

Few students of American history are aware that what is now the desolate Death Valley area was once a veritable Garden of Eden, complete with majestic palm trees and a proud people of heroic proportions.

In the June, 1970, issue of *Wild West* magazine, Ed Earl Repp told of the "honor and privilege" which was his in working with H. Flagler Cowden and his brother Charles C. Cowden, scientists "dedicated to the study of desert antiquity." Repp was present when the Cowden brothers uncovered the skeletal remains of a "human being believed to be the largest and oldest ever found in the United States."

It was in 1898, according to Repp, that the Cowdens discovered the human fossil remains of a giant female, "who was a member of the race of unprecedented large primitives which vanished from the face of the earth some 100,000 years ago." Although the scientists of that time did not have our modern dating methods, Repp states that the Cowdens were able to reach conclusions of time and age by the amount of silica in the soil and sands and by the state of petrification of the skeletal remains, along with the crystallization and opalization of the bone marrow.

"In the same earth strata where the giant female skeleton was found," Repp recalled, "they also recovered the remains of prehis-

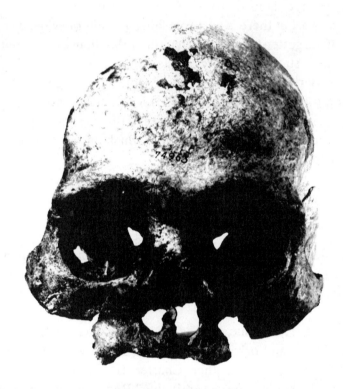

Alas, poor Calaveras Skull, we have come to know you well! On February 15, 1866, at a depth of 130 feet, James Mattison's gold mine shaft struck what he believed to be a root of petrified tree. Once the lime deposits had been removed from the object, J. C. Schribner, a merchant of Angel's Camp, California, was startled to find that he held a human skull in his hands. If the skull is truly that of a human who lived in the Pliocene period, then it would be somewhere in the neighborhood of ten million years old.

toric camels and mammals of . . . an elephantlike creature with four tusks instead of the present-day two. With them were the remains of petrified palm trees, towering ferns and prehistoric fishlife."

The Amerindians were not an abnormally tall people by any means. The Shoshones, Paiutes, Cosos and other desert tribes that occupied the valley at the time of the European invasion of the continent would have been dwarfs in comparison with the unknown race of prehistoric giants. If we may assume the same kind of height ratio with which we are familiar between the sexes then we might suppose that the men of the vanished valley paradise must have been eight feet tall.

Neither Neanderthal nor Cro-Magnon were taller than *Homo sapiens*. Who were these mysterious Goliaths of Death Valley?

Repp tells us that in the same pit in which the Cowdens found the skeleton of the giant female they unearthed the petrified remains of marine life, indicating that Death Valley may have been an inlet of the Pacific Ocean at the time the lost race of giants lived there. That the people were tall is further indicated by the discovery of "handhewn caves high up in the chalklike cliffs, almost inaccessible from either top or bottom approaches."

Repp writes that the Cowdens discovered a number of anomalous physical appendages and attributes not found in contemporary man. There were ". . . the existence of several extra 'buttons' at the base of the spine . . . and every indication betraying the woman and her people were endowed with a tail-like appendage. In her jaws, the canine teeth were twice the size in length than modern man."

The Cowdens theorized that when the California which we know today was formed, together with the rising of mountains and the retreat of the sea, the tropical climate left the valley regions. The steaming swamps were replaced by vast wastelands, which still remain over much of the southern portion of the state. Then, with the advent of the Ice Age ". . . the freezing northern blasts swept down upon the tropical beasts and humans, who wore little or no clothing, and literally froze them to death in their tracks. . . . The glacial icepacks moved down into Death Valley . . . at the rate of 4½ miles per hour, burying all life beneath layer-upon-layer of petrifying silt and glacial mud."

The fossilized remains of the seven and one-half foot woman were found at a depth of five feet in a "hard-rock formation of conglomerate containing small amounts of silica, which required longer time to petrify than normal desert sands."

A Prehistoric Amazon in California

Perhaps prehistoric California was the home of the Amazons, those legendary, statuesque female warriors; for in July, 1895, a party of miners working near Bridlevale Falls found the tomb of a woman whose skeletal remains indicated that she had stood six feet, eight inches in height.

G. F. Martindale, who was in charge of the miners, noticed a pile of stones that seemed to have been placed against the wall of a cliff in an unnatural formation. Assuming the rock had been stacked by human hands, Martindale told his men to begin removing the stones in order to investigate what might lie beyond the formation.

The miners were astonished when they found a wall of rock that had been shaped and fitted together with apparent knowledge of masonry. The joints between the blocks were all of a uniform eighth-of-an-inch thickness, and a contemporary news account quoted one of the men as stating that the stonework was ". . . beautiful . . . as pretty as any wall on any building that I have ever seen."

The miners felt at first that they might have stumbled upon some lost treasure trove, and they set about tearing down the wall so that they might claim their found wealth.

Instead of riches beyond their wildest imaginings, however, the men found a large mummified corpse lying on a ledge that had been carved from the natural stone. The miners lighted their carbide head lamps and attempted to translate their disappointment into a more profitable examination of the burial vault, but all the chamber contained was the mummy of a very large woman. The corpse had been wrapped in animal skins and covered with a fine gray powder. She was clutching a child to her breast.

When the mummy was taken to Los Angeles, scientists there agreed that the woman was the citizen of a race that had thrived on this continent long before the American Indian had become dominant. They further arrived at a consensus that the woman's height of six feet, eight inches would have represented a height in life of at least seven feet. Figuring the classic height difference between men and women, they supposed that the males of the forgotten species would have been nearly eight feet tall.

A Catacomb of Goliaths in North Carolina

A veritable catacomb of the skeletal remains of this lost race of giants was found when workmen were opening a way for the railroad between Wildon and Garrysburg, North Carolina. According to a contemporary newspaper account dated April 4, 1874, the bodies exhumed were of a "strange and remarkable formation."

> The skulls were nearly an inch in thickness; the teeth were filed sharp, as those of cannibals, enamel perfectly preserved; the bones were of wonderful strength, the femur being as long as the leg of an ordinary man, the stature of the body being probably as great as eight or nine feet. Near their heads were sharp stone arrows, some mortars . . . and the bowls of pipes, apparently of soft soapstone. The teeth of the skeletons are said to be as large as those of a horse.
>
> The bodies were found closely packed together, laid tier on tier, as it seemed. There was no discernible ingress or egress to the mound. The mystery is, who these were, to what race they belonged, to what era, and how they came to be buried there. To these enquiries no answer has yet been made, and meantime the ruthless spade continues to cleave body and soul asunder, throwing up in mangled masses the bones of this heroic tribe. It is hoped that some effort will be made to preserve authentic and accurate accounts of

these discoveries, and to throw some light, if possible, on the lost tribe whose bones are thus rudely disturbed from their sleep in earth's bosom.

Daily Independent, Helena Montana

An Unknown Race of Goliaths in Texas

The *Dallas Morning News*, July 30, 1974, carried yet another account of the discovery of a seven-foot woman. Frank X. Tolbert stated that Dr. Ernest (Bull) Adams, an attorney in Somervell County and an amateur archaeologist, found her bones sealed in a cave at the crest of a high mesa near the hamlet of Chalk Mountain. The complete skeleton of the woman, which Dr. Adams discovered sometime in the middle 1950s, was placed on display in a glass case in the Somervell County Museum on the courthouse square in Glen Rose, Texas.

Dr. Adams believed that the woman was of average size for her unknown race and that ". . . the cave was a maternity ward for these giants . . . the cave was steam-heated by water boiled under the floor . . . the woman had died in childbirth apparently. And her perfect teeth suggested she was quite young."

Skeletons of Gigantic Humans in Wisconsin

The *New York Times* for May 4, 1912, told of a find of several skeletons of gigantic humans made while excavating a mound at Lake Delavan, Wisconsin. news of the discovery was brought to Madison, Wisconsin, by Maurice Morrissey, who, in turn, informed the curator of the State Historical Museum. According to the newspaper account, eighteen skeletons were found in one large mound at a Lake Lawn farm:

The heads, presumably those of men, are much larger than the heads of any race which inhabit America today. From directly over the eyesockets, the head slopes straight back and the nasal bones protrude far above the cheekbones. The jawbones are long and pointed, bearing a minute resemblance to the head of a monkey. The teeth in front of the jaw are regular molars.

There were also found in the mounds the skeletons, presumably of women, which had smaller heads, but were similar in facial characteristics. The skeletons were embedded in charcoal and covered over with layers of baked clay to shed water from the sepulchre.

Tennessee's Mysterious Coffins of Wee Folk

No sooner must we confront the question of the identity of this mysterious race of lost giants than we discover that the skeletal remains of people less than two feet tall have also been discovered on this continent. We may almost feel cheated that we must remain so totally ignorant of so wonderfully diverse a range of cultures and peoples who have flourished in this land in a world before our own.

Harper's Magazine, July, 1869, stated that Tennessee newspapers for the year 1828 told of several burying grounds, from a half acre to an acre in extent, which were discovered in Sparta, White County, Tennessee, in which extremely small people had been interred in tiny stone coffins. The tallest of the wee folk discovered was 19 inches.

Lest one think that those who discovered the strange burying ground had merely found an infant cemetery for the giants, contemporary accounts describe the bones of the small ones to have been "strong and well set, and the whole frames well formed."

The graves were only dug about two feet deep, and the tiny corpses had been buried with their heads to the east, laid on their backs, with their hands folded across their chests. In the bend of the left arm of each skeleton lay a pint vessel made of ground stone or shell of a grayish color. Each vessel contained two or three shells. The skeletons were regular and uniform, with the exception of one that bore 94 pearl beads about its neck.

According to *Harper's Magazine*, a work published in 1853, *The Romance of Natural History*, also refers to diminutive sarcophagi that were found in Kentucky and Tennessee.

Nearly everyone loves a mystery, but most people desire an eventual solution to prevent their being driven mad from frustration over the lack of any contributive clues. What once seemed a neat, progressive, evolutionary line has become hopelessly convoluted and chaotic. While many archaeologists and anthropologists are debating the origins of the Amerindian and the date of his arrival on this continent, few choose to pursue the erratic path dotted with the skeletal remains of giants— some of whom might even have had tails— and the evidence that this continent appears to have supported "worlds upon worlds" before any "Adam" of our epoch set foot on these shores.

New World? Bah! Humbug! Civilizations have flourished and have been devastated on this continent many times in an unknown past—perhaps before Egypt was more than a dream and long before Greece constructed her first city-state.

V

Mysterious Master Builders

The most permanent kind of evidence that advanced civilizations thrived in man's prehistory may be seen in the vast number of architectural and engineering wonders that are scattered throughout the globe. The walls and buildings of some incredibly old cities have been found constructed of blocks so large that even today our most powerful and massive transports and derricks would find it impossible to hoist them and fit them into place with any degree of efficiency. Yet, orthodox archaeologists would have us believe that primitive peoples could accomplish the task easily enough with vine ropes and wooden block and tackle.

Tiahuanaco — City of Wonders

Tiahuanaco, the "City of the Dead," flourished long before the more intelligent of the Incas decided to put one stone on top of another and fashion a crude hut. According to Incan legends, Tiahuanaco was built by a race of giants, whose fatherland had been destroyed in a great deluge that had lasted for two months. These powerful survivors transported remnants of their culture to Tiahuanaco on the shores of Lake Titicaca in Bolivia's high plateau. If Egypt was the principal colony of Atlantis in the Old World, then

The Sacred Lake and Tothmes Pylon in Karnak.

Tiahuanaco might well have been one of the sunken continent's attempt at rebirth in the New World.

In his expedition of 1932, Wendell Bennett found evidence indicating that the city is at least 5,000 years old. But it was a German archaeologist, Arthur Posnansky, who first recognized the significance of Tiahuanaco as a pre-Columbian culture of major importance. The scholar became so impressed by the city that he became a Bolivian citizen so that he might devote nearly half a century to research in the mysterious city. Posnansky's studies convinced him that Tiahuanaco was older than any city on the South American continent, perhaps 10,000 to 20,000 years old.

In Posnansky's opinion, later to be re-echoed by others, the high plateau had once been much closer to sea level than its present altitude of 13,000 feet. The German archaeologist theorized that a terrible cataclysm in comparatively recent geological time might have caused a gigantic upheaval that had raised the entire area. Although these changes in the earth's crust did not swallow the city or destroy it, the change in climate and altitude had made it a less desirable place to live and the inhabitants had left voluntarily.

Arthur Posnansky died in 1946 before he could completely unravel the enigma of the lost citizens of Tiahuanaco, but he was convinced that he had traced their influence on the native culture as far north as the coastal deserts of Peru and as far south as Argentina. In the view of the German archaeologist, the differences between Tiahuanaco and other pre-Columbian cultures were many and significant. The citizens of Tiahuanaco were taller and had distinctive facial characteristics quite apart from the high-cheekboned visages of today's dwellers of the high plateau.

But the most startling tale told by the few artifacts left in the city is of a New World civilization that was amazingly similar to that of ancient Egypt.

The *Calassassayax* (house of worship) is so similar to the Egyptian temple of Karnak in design and layout that its relative dimensions make it almost a scale model of the Old World structure.

The majestic Columns of Hypostyle Hall located in the mystical city of Karnak.

The stones used in the *Calassassayax* are fitted and joined with their joints and facing parts polished to make it a nearly perfect match. The Incas did not build in such a manner, but the ancient Egyptians did.

The surgeons of Tiahuanaco were skilled in trepanning the brain, as were the Egyptians physicians. Posnansky uncovered skulls with well-healed bone grafts, which offered silent testimony to the skill of the ancient doctors and their knowledge of anatomy.

While assigned to the U.S. Army Mission in La Paz, Bolivia, Neil Richards excavated the nearby ruins of Tiahuanaco.

"The Tiahuanacans' copper trepanning instruments are identical to those used by the Egyptians," Richards writes. "The credibility of 'cultural credence' is stretched considerably when related to brain operations. It is possible to accept the fact that two cultures may have developed a form of brain operation (although few did) but that both cultures used identical instruments and methods seems unusual to say the least. The instruments are of high grade copper and include drills and chisels. In themselves they indicate an advanced degree of metallurgy, knowledge of simple machinery, and development of surgical practices far more detailed than can be expected in primitive societies."

Another aspect of Tiahuanacan culture has puzzled those who have investigated its ruins. Many of the buildings were constructed of massive, finished stones, many tons in weight, that have been placed in such a manner that only a people with advanced engineering methods could have designed and transported them. If this were not enough of an impossible situation, the particular andesite used in much of the Tiahuanacan construction can only be found in a quarry that lies 50 miles away in the mountains.

Because of the many cultural similarities between Egypt and Tiahuanaco, some bold scholars have suggested that there must have been contact between the two civilizations. A few archaeologists have even dared hypothesize that Tiahuanaco might have antedated Egypt, and its culture may have spread to the Old World in some manner not yet realized.

As far as this author can determine, no archaeologist with a professional standing to jeopardize has announced his theory that Tiahuanaco and ancient Egypt may have drawn their similarities from a common source, a prehistoric civilization that antedated both and colonized both.

The Marvelous Mountain Fortress of Sacsahuaman

The Peruvian city of Sacsahuaman presents similar problems. This great walled citadel crouches on top of a cone-shaped hill 12,000 feet above sea-level. Its vast residential palaces, storehouses, inner forts, paved courtyards, and 50,000-gallon reservoir present a persistent puzzle to architects and engineers. The Incas are given credit for having constructed Sacsahuaman during the fifteenth century, but even the guidebooks state that the "basic structure" may have been there, lying in ruins, awaiting new inhabitants, when the Incas claimed the lofty fortress city.

Conventional archaeology and Hollywood epics have conditioned us to accept the image of hundreds of half-naked slaves tugging and pushing at massive building blocks to avoid the lash of brutal overseers. If such man-power fashioned the citadel of Sacsahuaman, then the mountain trails must have been crowded indeed. The quarries that yielded the stone for Sacsahuaman are located nine to 20 miles from the city. Some of the boulders are estimated at more than 200 tons, and the largest is 12 feet thick and 25 feet tall.

Does it not boggle the mind to envision thousands of slaves and harnessed llamas tugging such massive boulders over rivers, down deep ravines, then up the mountain-top site of Sacsahuaman?

Such an image becomes ludicrous to the most devout and orthodox thinkers. Our most modern earth-moving machinery would be dwarfed by such boulders, but given our contemporary technology our heaviest machinery, and an enormous electrical power plant, our engineers could probably duplicate the giant mountain fortress of Sacsahuaman. Conventional archaeologists, however, are not prepared to grant those poor, tugging, semi-ignorant savages the wheel, let alone electricity, earth-moving machinery, and modern industrial knowledge.

Some archaeologists, in unconscious vast understatement, have theorized that the Incas were skilled stone-cutters, who quarried and fashioned thousands of boulders to that no two were alike and so that they could fit together perfectly without cement. In Sacsahuaman, the stones fit together so precisely that a machinist's thickness gauge cannot be inserted between the rocks in the walls.

M. K. Jessup once observed in a presentation of the mystery of Sacsahuaman that tones can be worked *in situ* to fit closely together, that is, stones roughly cut can be shaped to fit by being rubbed together.

"Some Peruvians believe that a chemical may have been used to soften the surfaces of the stone for quick-wearing," Jessup commented. "However, to say that the stones were worn to fit does not explain how these megaliths, weighing tons apiece, were handled. It is clearly impossible for the Indians to have pushed and pulled these stones into the desired shapes. No satisfactory answer to this problem has been found."

And, we might add, no satisfactory answer probably ever will be found until archaeologists are willing to entertain the suggestion that throughout the world ancient civilizations reflect the unforgettable glory of an advanced antediluvian proto-civilization. The glory that was Greece, the grandeur that was Rome, the mystery that was Egypt may be little more than semi-literate barbarians self-consciously emulating the magnificence that was Atlantis, the prehistoric seed from which the cultures that form our own epoch sprouted.

Feats of Prehistoric Technology

If there was not an advanced prehistoric technology in some humanistic wheel of cyclical civilization, how can we explain primitive peoples with only pulleys, twisted vines, and reed baskets constructing the following architectural and engineering marvels?

The Magnificent Inca Roads: Victor Von Hagen, for the American Geographical Society, discovered a 15-mile stretch of highway as carefully engineered as anything the Romans, who had the wheel, ever built. Maps indicated two highways nearly the length of South America, supplemented by an elaborate system of secondary routs. A main trunk highway runs for 2,700 miles, beginning in Columbia, running south through Ecuador, Peru, and Bolivia, splitting down to reach Argentina and Chile.

The Mayans' superhighway: The National Geographic Society and Tulane University unearthed a raised thoroughfare, easily the equivalent of a modern superhighway. Although it is known that the Mayans were ignorant of the wheel and did not employ dray animals, archaeologists have decreed that the elaborate thoroughfares were constructed to serve as trade routs for commerce transported on the backs of slaves. This, of course, means that those slaves who were not carrying 200-ton boulders up mountainsides were free to trot along the superhighway with fish and fodder on their backs.

The Baalbeck Platforms: This incredible group of temples in Syria is noteworthy for the 54 eight-foot-wide and 90-foot-tall pillars that support flat stone slabs estimated to weight 1,200 tons each. Modern engineers have admitted that no contemporary derrick could hoist such an incredible weight to a height of 90 feet without collapsing in a scatter of screaming iron. Yet the textbooks dictate that lash-driven slaves managed to plop those 1,200-ton stone slabs on top of those tall pillars.

India's Black Pagoda: On top of a 228-foot-high temple rests a single stone slab, 25 feet thick, with an estimated weight of 2,000 tons. The brain boils attempting to conjecture the ingenious pulley system or series of platforms or thousands of slaves required to move a four-million-pound monolith to a perch 228 feet above the ground.

The Great Cheops Pyramid

The Great Cheops Pyramid covers 13 acres and is 481 feet high and 756 feet wide at each side of its square base. Certainly the tallest

The wondrous pyramids at Giza as they appear at night under colorful illumination.

structure in antiquity, the Cheops Pyramid, discounting a number of skyscrapers in the United States, still ranks as the ninth tallest architectural marvel in the world today. It has been estimated that more than 2,300,000 stone blocks of an average weight of two and one-half tons went into the construction of this last resting place for the Pharaoh Cheops, circa 2800 B.C.

The Pyramid of Khafre, near Cheops, stands 442 feet high and covers 12 acres. The third pyramid in the massive triumvirate, Mycerinus, is 215 feet tall and 346 feel wide on each side.

Science writer Otto Binder states that the classic picture of teams of men roped together and tugging away at moving the massive stone blocks up the ramps, tier by tier, may be feasible, but such a method of construction would call for such unlikely figures as 100,000 slaves struggling in torment for 20 years to shape one pyramid.

"Could any governing agency, no matter how tyrannical and all-powerful, ever conscript that many workers over that long a period of time without (A) causing a revolt, (B) draining off too much manpower from other tasks, notably raising food, (C) being unable to sell the populace on why the pyramid was necessary in the first place," Binder wonders.

"Built openly as tombs for the dead Pharaohs . . . would not even the most cowed and oppressed people question how worthwhile this goal was? Especially when brothers, fathers, neighbors, friends were whisked away in chains and brutally whipped while dragging at the ropes, so that most of them died in a few years from sheer overwork? It would seem that modern archaeologists and sociologists are assuming gross errors in mass psychology when they blandly state that each pyramid was built at the cost of 100,000 lives without protest . . . Ancient Egypt, with a population of only a few millions, could hardly stand that fearful drain of numbers for long periods of ten or twenty years. . . ."

With Cairo, Egypt, as his backdrop, Brad Steiger pauses to relax and consider his next area of investigation.

Alien Pyramid Builders

Binder and certain UFOlogists have suggested the intervention of "alien pyramid builders" who used the power plants of their flying saucers to hoist such tonnage into place. M. K. Jessup, in one of his writings of the UFO enigma, stated his belief that a spaceship of vast proportions may have brought colonists to various parts of the earth and may also have supplied the heavy lift power for erecting great stone works before it was suddenly destroyed or taken away.

Science writer Joseph Goodavage has theorized that the antediluvians may have controlled the secret of raw power, an elemental force, which enabled them to erect such astounding edifices. "The evidence suggests that something interrupted the construction of most of these ancient buildings," Goodavage states; "almost universally, the original builders disappeared and left no trace whatever of their real identify.

"Theorem (1): This 'power' was levitation, the ability to reverse and control gravity.

"Theorem (2): The beings who used this power to build these structures in antediluvian times were extraterrestrial in origin.

"Theorem (3): For some undetermined reason, they were unable or unwilling to leave Earth for a predetermined time. When they did leave, some of their constructions were left unfinished."

Mystery Ground Figures

From Canada to Baja, California, dozens of giant ground figures formed by rows of stones or shallow trenches and ranging from 200 to 500 feet long have been spotted by aircraft flying over desert regions of the western United States. The designs of the ground figures form loops, concentric circles, rectangles, and serpents. Authorities assign a date of about A.D. 1000 to the figures and declare that they resulted from some important kind of undetermined group activity.

Because of scientific interest in the Richat Formation on the edge of the Sahara desert in West Africa, the 30-mile circle of concentric ridges was made a priority item for photography by Majors McDivitt and White on their Gemini space flight. The astronauts' photographs emphasized the astounding symmetry of the structure, which scientists have classified as some kind of geological phenomenon, rather than a man-made mystery.

Commercial airliners flying over the desert near Nasca, Peru, were among the first to report the giant animals and ornaments that cover an area of at least 40 square miles. It was not until 1941 that archaeologists began a systematic mapping of the area and the strange pathways were discovered to be more than prehistoric agricultural furrows. Scholars have been hard put to explain how an ancient race could have projected such intricate patterns with such a wide area when, from the ground, only one or two lines can be seen at one time. Modern archaeologists, employing the most sophisticated methods known today, found that they had to spend as many as three days mapping out on paper faithful reproductions of some of the figures.

As to why primitive peoples would go to such great physical lengths to construct such nonutilitarian ground figures, researcher James Moseley has suggested that the figures, clearly visible and meaningful only from the air, might have been formed by a prehistoric people who had a means of traveling by air.

"Or more likely," Moseley writes, "earth-bound themselves, they constructed their huge markings as signals to interplanetary visitors or to some advanced earth race that occasionally visited them."

Fantastic as these suggestions may seem, such theories cannot be discarded until, or unless, some other account is given for the size of the desert patterns.

Whether or not the prehistoric scientists, architects, and engineers who fashioned the marvels in stone which we have examined in this chapter also had heavier-than-air powered vehicles is, perhaps, a foolish kind of academic question, for the stalwarts of orthodox science are by no means prepared to grant us more than a great deal of slave labor in antiquity and noting ore in man's prehistory than fierce hunters and low-browed cave dwellers. If, however, the reader's rational mind should require an advanced, technologically proficient construction crew to place a 2,000-ton slab atop a 228-foot pagoda in Indian rather a 100,000 slaves tugging on a vine rope pulley system . . . wheeled vehicles to travel a 2,7000-mile-long South American highway rather than merchants and porters transporting trade items on their backs . . . a type of aircraft plotting out the Nasca lines rather than the huge ground figures resulting from some undetermined religiously oriented group activity, then he may be prepared to concede that when man, as we know him in our epoch, was just beginning to think about clustering together to form a rudimentary village, some previous human, or hominid, civilization was desperately trying to pound a bit of knowledge into our ancestors' thick skulls so that their great antediluvian culture should not have flowered in vain. And surely, to our ancestors at the beginning of our epoch, these men with their wonderful machines and mechanical devices would have seemed like gods.

Donnelly's Artifacts

Ignatius Donnelly wrote his monumental study of Atlantis in 1882 and airplanes and automobiles did not figure in his vision of the vanished continent's advanced civilization. Donnelly did, however, conceptualize the Atlanteans as being so intellectually and technologically superior to the ancients of the Mediterranean region that the Greeks would have regarded them as deities.

"The history of Atlantis is the key to the Greek mythology," he wrote. "There can be no question that these gods of Greece were human beings. The tendency to attach divine attributes to great earthly rulers is one deeply implanted in human nature."

It was, therefore, Donnelly's contention that the Greeks simply converted the kings and queens of Atlantis into gods and goddesses, which is why instead of a solar or nature worship, the Greece of antiquity had a lusty stable of deities who were born, ate, drank, made love, and died. Olympus was Atlantis.

Donnelly summarizes his proposition in seven main points:

"1. They (the gods) were not the makers, but the rulers of the world.

"2. They were human in their attributes; they loved, sinned, and fought battles, the very sites of which are given; they founded cities, and civilized the people of the shores of the Mediterranean.

"3. They dwelt upon an island in the Atlantis, 'in the remote west . . . where the sun shines after it has ceased to shine on Greece.'

"4. Their land was destroyed in a deluge.

"5. They were ruled over by Poseidon [god of the sea] and Atlas [who bears the world upon his shoulders].

"6. Their empire extended to Egypt and Italy and the shores of Africa, precisely as stated by Plato.

"7. They existed during the Bronze Age and at the beginning of the Iron Age."

The mediterranean peoples spoke of the Atlanteans as being possessed of great physical strength "so that the earth shook sometimes under their tread." Such an accolade could refer to the Atlanteans' earth-moving equipment, their use of explosives to clear highways through mountains, and their efficient manipulation of labor-saving devices.

The primitive Mediterraneans were also in awe of the Atlanteans' ability to move "through space without the loss of a moment of time." Such an allusion could speak of anything from their machine-driven ships to their aircraft. And, perhaps, an instantaneous method of transportation that lies as yet unexploited by our own science.

The Atlanteans were said to be "wise and able to communicate their wisdom to men." Such a god-like attribute may have been facilitated by exceptional linguistic ability or by telepathic faculty, but certainly testifies to their civilizing influence upon all with whom they came into contact.

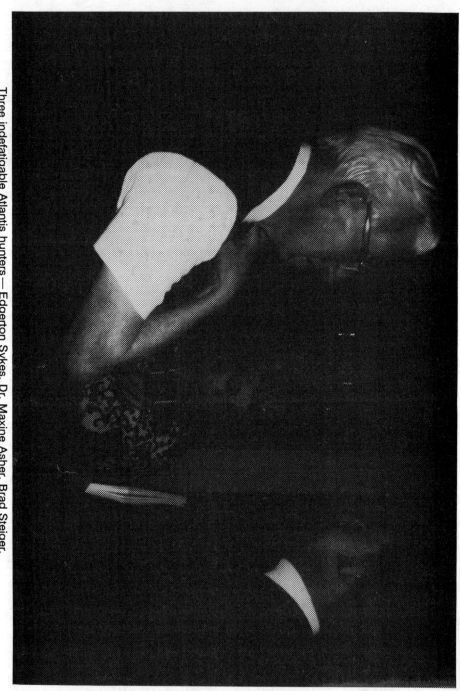

Three indefatigable Atlantis hunters — Edgerton Sykes, Dr. Maxine Asher, Brad Steiger.

Pre-Mayan Canal System in the Yucatan

Today's Mayan farmer employs the "milpa" or primitive "slash-and-burn" system of land usage. In this method, trees and jungle growth are burned away from prospective farmland. After the first rain, seed holes are drilled into the soft soil with a sharp stick. The land is cultivated for one more season, then the field is abandoned and a new clearing is burned in the jungle to provide land for the next crop.

Certain archaeologists have theorized that the slash-and-burn technique of clearing farmland may have been one of the factors that depleted the Mayan's land and precipitated a decline of their civilization some time around 900 A.D.

But just a few years ago, archaeologists uncovered a canal-reservoir system on the Yucatan peninsula in Mexico that indicates that an early, pre-Mayan culture supported an advanced knowledge of hydraulic engineering and provided its people with extensive agricultural benefits more than 2,000 years ago. Some unknown culture established a network of 30 canals and 25 man-made, large-scale reservoirs approximately 30 miles southeast of what is now the little capital city of Campeche on the Gulf of Mexico.

The archaeological excavators are from Brigham Young University, Provo, Utah, and it is their opinion, as they labor through the processes of mapping, surveying, excavating, and studying the site, that they have found what will be the "oldest and most intricate water-collection system in pre-Mayan history and possibly the only one of its kind in the New World."

Dr. Ray T. Matheny, associate professor of archaeology, credits the unknown canal builders as having been skilled engineers who were able to determine the difficult gradients that permitted rainwater to collect in canals and flow into waiting reservoirs.

Nelson Wadsworth, writing in *Science Digest*, March, 1974, quotes Dr. Matheny as stating: "What we are finding at [the ruins of] Edzna is a fairly large city of several hundred families organized on a high level of political authority and sustained by a stable economy which we believe was pot-water farming. This type of canal and rainwater collection for agriculture was simply not known elsewhere on the flat lands of the New World."

Dr. Matheny declares the site to be unique because of the deep soils which are rare on the Yucatan peninsula, together with the possible use of canals for pot-watering. Such intensive agricultural techniques are not generally known or practiced by the Mayan people of today.

The archaeologists found that rainwater from the adjacent jungle still drains into the huge feeder canal, then flows into a moat surrounding a fortress before it moves into a number of nearby reservoirs. The team from Brigham Young measured the canal as 12 kilometers long, and in some areas, 50 meters wide.

Dr. Matheny commented: "This in itself was a tremendous construction achievement. It could not have been built without some kind of advanced engineering know-how and sophisticated social organization."

An Awesome System of Subterranean Aqueducts in Iran

Although there is no mystery about who constructed the 170,000 miles of underground channels in Iran more than 3,000 years ago, the system of subterranean aqueducts is an awesome achievement that still provides 75 percent of the water used in that country today.

With the exception of areas in the northwestern provinces and the southern shores of the Caspian Sea, Iran receives only six to ten inches of rainfall each year. But far from being a barren, scorched region, Iran has been a self-sufficient agricultural nation of centuries. It has been able to grow its own food, and it has managed to produce crops or export by tapping underground water through the means of an ingenious system called *qanat* (from a Semitic word, "to dig").

H. E. Wulff explained the system in the April, 1968, issue of *Scientific American*: "The qanat system consists of underground channels that convey water from aquifers in highlands to the surface at lower levels by gravity. . . The qanat works of Iran were built on a scale that rivaled the great aqueducts of the Roman Empire. Whereas the Roman aqueducts now are only historical curiosity, the Iranian system is still in use after 3,000 years and has continually been expanded. . . ."

The qanat shafts may go as deep as 300 feet to reach water, and such depths require windlasses at intervals of 100 feet apart. Guide shafts are sunk at intervals of about 300 yards to indicate the route and the pitch of the conduit for the well diggers. The mouth end of the conduit is lined with stones to protect it from storm-water damage. The tunnels and shafts need no reinforcement when they have been dug through hard clay or a coarse conglomerate that is well-packed.

"Not until the qanat has been completed and has operated for some time is it possible to determine whether it will be a continuous 'runner' or a seasonal source that provides water only in the spring or after heavy rains," writes Wulff.

The initial investment in construction of a qanat is considerable, and the owners and builders will often result to laborious devices in order to insure or enlarge its yield. Careful attention is also given to maintenance of the qanat.

"As is to be expected of a system that has existed for thousands of years and is so important to the life of the nation, the buildings of qanats and the distribution of water are ruled by laws and common understandings that are hallowed by tradition," Wulff states.

"The builders of a qanat must obtain the consent of the owners of the land it will cross, but permission cannot be refused arbitrarily. It must be granted if the new qanat will not interfere with the yield from an existing qanat, which usually means that the distance between the two must be several hundred yards, depending on the geological formation involved."

California's Mysterious Stone Walls

As regards the mysterious walls of the Berkeley and Oakland hills in California, no one seems to have the foggiest idea who built them so that their line of progression is not at all "ruled by laws and common understandings that are hallowed by tradition."

The rather ordinary-looking stone walls are found mainly in heavily wooded or chaparral-covered areas. Although in a few places it appears as if they might have been utilized as some kind of fortification, they seem to fulfill none of the usual functions of walls.

Sibley S. Morrill investigated the matter of the perplexing walls for the October, 1972, issue of *Pursuit*. According to his research, the walls survive in sections ranging from 20 feet to more than 200 yards in length. In height, they vary from two feet or less to five feet or a bit more. Their breadth at ground level is a rather impressive four feet. In Morrill's opinion, such breadth makes it ". . . a near certainty that the walls originally were much higher through the use of smaller stones along the top."

Limited digging near the base indicates that the rock goes down about ten inches below the surface. It is difficult to imagine the wall serving any nonfunctional purpose, since some of the rocks employed in their construction weigh more than 200 pounds.

A Mr. Seth Simpson of Oakland is said to have studied the walls as a hobby for a good many years. According to Simpson, the walls extend for nearly seven miles south into the Oakland hills, but he has not been able to relate them to any known boundary markings:

"Water company survey maps show that none of the walls has any detectable relationship to boundary lines; except for one case in the Vollmer Peak area, boundary lines parallel no walls nearer than about 600 yards."

Neither does any clue remain to suggest that they might be the remains of any sort of animal pen or corral.

"They are, for the most part, straight," Morrill informs us. "Some intersect at an angle, and there are instances of parallel walls separated by as much as ten yards or so, but there are no indications whatsoever that they formed enclosures."

In the hills behind Milpitas, Simpson discovered similar walls in a gently rolling, almost treeless country.

Again, with only one exception, "they offer no suggestion of the usual purpose for a wall. . . . The walls are virtually useless as fences. . . . In the Milpitas area, the stone walls just run their way for a few score or a few hundred yards and then stop."

No area resident appears to know anything about the origin of the walls. The walls have just always been there.

An examination of old newspaper clippings concerning the reactions of various residents of the area to the builders' wall reveal opinions ranging from Mexican to Chinese, from pioneers to "Mazatlánes," sounding "strangely similar to Atlanteans, to whom the Aztecs and their predecessors, who lived about Mazatlán, down the Mexican coast, were reputed to be related."

Seth Simpson concedes that it is possible that at least some of the walls might have been built by Indians for the purpose of driving game into "a sort of cul-de-sac where they could be easily killed."

Simpson also states that, in the absence of extensive excavations along the walls, such a theory is all he can suggest: "They were built by unknown persons, in an unknown year, for an unknown purpose. And very possibly, despite our hopes, they will remain a puzzle for an indefinite future."

A "Curious Wall" in Jordan

The London *Daily Telegraph* for January 27, 1973, provided the details of another puzzling wall that appeared to go nowhere for no particular reason.

The recorder of this mystery wall was the eminent Sir Alec Kirkbride, who, at age 75, was identified by the *Daily Telegraph* as one of the last surviving British officers to have fought in the Arab revolt with the famous Lawrence of Arabia. Kirkbride's wall runs for 20 miles at a distance of about 12 miles from Petra to Jordan.

One of Brad Steiger's favorite places of mystery — the ancient Nabatean city of Petra, located in what is now the country of Jordan.

Sir Alec, who was for many years British Resident in Transjordan and terminated his long career as British Ambassador in Libya, informed the press that he first spotted the "curious wall" when he flew over it in a light airplane. He was so intrigued that he returned to take a closer look from horseback.

"It was utterly staggering," Sir Alec recalled., "because it had involved a tremendous amount of labor, being about ten feet wide and two feet tall. But it bore no relation to any boundary or defensive position at all. It's just a great jumble."

Sir Alec's theory is that the wall was built by Nabateans in the early Christian era, but he admitted that he is far from convinced that those desert peoples really did construct the mystery wall. "Despite much research, no one can explain it," he commented.

In the April, 1973, issue of *Pursuit*, a staff writer offered the following observation regarding Sir Alec's desert wall to nowhere:

". . . Sir Alec, who certainly knows the area as well as anyone can, states flatly that this wall is not a defensive or boundary wall. In fact, its dimensions make it sound more like a road; but the description suggests that it doesn't go anywhere. If all this is so, and our figures are correct, it means that some group of (presumably demented) people carefully piled up 2,112 cubic feet of rock for no reason whatsoever. . . . One cannot seriously entertain the idea that people lugged stones around for the fun of it, particularly in the inhospitable area around Petra."

VI

The Enigma
Of The
Great Pyramid

Is it possible to determine the precise date of the end of the world by utilizing certain calculations derived from the Great Pyramid of Giza?

Is it true that the "pyramid inch" is equal to a year in prophecy?

Were the pyramids built by architects from Atlantis?

Or from some extraterrestrial source?

Is the Great Pyramid of Cheops the physical embodiment of a lost science of vast antiquity and unsurpassed knowledge?

Although everyone who has pursued the matter of pyramids to any degree is able to agree that the Great Pyramid is at least 4,000 years old, further assertions as to who built it, when, and why are certain to encounter opposing theories.

As to *what* the Great Pyramid is, Peter Tompkins in his *Secrets of the Great Pyramid* states that it has been established that it is a ". . . carefully located geodetic marker, or fixed landmark, on which the geography of the ancient world was brilliantly constructed; that it served as a celestial observatory from which maps and tables of the stellar hemisphere could be accurately drawn; and that it incorporates in its sides and angles the means for creating a highly sophisticated map projection of the northern hemisphere. It is, in

The enigmatic Sphinx and the Great Pyramid at Giza.

fact, a scale model of the hemisphere, correctly incorporating the geographical degree of latitude and longitude."

A Repository of a Universal System of Weights and Measures

Tompkins hypothesizes that the Great Pyramid may well be the "repository of an ancient and possibly universal system of weights and measures, the model for the most sensible system of linear and temporal measurements available on earth, based on the polar axis of rotation . . . whose accuracy is now confirmed by the mensuration of orbiting satellites."

Until quite recently, there was no proof that the ancient Egyptians had any of their number capable of planning or constructing such a magnificent edifice as the Great Pyramid. But now, according to Tompkins, it is quite clear that whoever built the Great Pyramid "knew the precise circumference of the planet, and the length of the year to several decimals — data which were not rediscovered till the seventeenth century. Its architects may well have known the mean length of the earth's orbit round the sun, the specific density of the planet, the 26,000 year cycle of the equinoxes, the acceleration of gravity and the speed of light."

Even today with our skyscrapers reaching for the clouds in all of our major cities, the Great Pyramid is still the world's most massive building. And only in this recent generation of man has the Great Pyramid been surpassed as the world's tallest building. The Empire State Building in New York City is among the very highest buildings ever erected by modern man, yet it is only about two-fifths the volume of the Great Pyramid.

The Great Pyramid is the only remaining "wonder" of the seven legendary marvels of the ancient world.* With the remarkable

---

*The others: the gardens of Semiramis at Babylon, the statue of the Olympian Zeus by Phidias, the temple of Artemis at Ephesus, the mausoleum at Halicarnassus, the Colossus of Rhodes, and the Pharos (lighthouse) at Alexandria. In some listings the Walls of Babylon are substituted for the Alexandrian Pharos.

endurance which is displays, it may be the only wonder remaining after our epoch has had its play.

A Master Builder of a "Different Race"

Who was the master builder who drew the plans for this architectural marvel? It would appear that the architect for this greatest of Egyptian pyramids was not even an Egyptian. His name spelled in Egyptian is Khufu. The Greeks called him Cheops. But according to the third-century Egyptian historian Manetho, Khufu was "of a different race."

The famous fifth-century Greek historian Herodotus states that the builders of the Great Pyramids were *shepherds*.

This seems all the stranger when Genesis tells us that to the Egyptians "every shepherd is an abomination." The Egyptians employed others to tend to their flocks and herds.) Yet according to many records, Khufu, or Cheops, the master builder of the Great Pyramid, was a shepherd.

Some Bible students will immediately recall that the Pharaohs who ruled during the Israelites' Egyptian sojourn set them to building pyramids. Since the Israelites were a nation of shepherds, could Khufu have been an Israelite architect who designed the Great Pyramid before Moses led the enslaved hosts on their exodus?

It would seem unlikely, for the pyramid at Giza was constructed much earlier than the Israelites' Egyptian Period, and the pyramids that the children of Israel tugged and heaved together are deemed to be rather shoddy and hastily erected duplicates of the Pyramid of Cheops.

In a paper published by Ambassador College, Herman L. Hoeh assembled some interesting data, together with some remarkable hypotheses, which may present a clearer portrait of the enigmatic architect of the Great Pyramid.

Cheops was not a polytheist, for Herodotus records that he closed the temples and prohibited the Egyptians from offering sacrifices. The deity whom Cheops served was named "Amen" in the ancient

Brad Steiger at the tomb in the King's Chamber of the Great Pyramid.

Egyptian spelling. Strange as it may seem, Hoeh reminds us, "one of the names of Jesus Christ, from the Hebrew, is 'Amen.' " (Revelation 3:14)

Joseph, the wise Israelite visionary and dream interpreter, who was sold into Egyptian captivity by his jealous brothers, rose to prominence under the Pharaoh of Upper Egypt, who was named Amenemhet III. Because "Amen" appears to have been a common name among the Pharaohs in Joseph's day, Hoeh maintains that the rulers must have been strongly influenced by the religion of Cheops.

Hoeh finds additional fuel to fire his hypothesis of Creator-inspired Cheops in that Pharaoh Amenemhet gave Joseph "to wife Asenath the daughter of Potipherah priest of On" (Genesis 31:45). On is but another name for the god Amen, states Hoeh, and he goes on to point out that in Revelation 1:8, in the original, inspired text of this verse, "the Greek word that Christ used was 'On' — 'the existing one'!"

Hoeh's research convinces him that Cheops was a contemporary King Zoser of Egypt (1737-1818 B.C.), who built the "step pyramid" a short time before Cheops constructed the Great Pyramid. Zoser ruled part of Lower Egypt while Joseph served as Prime Minister under Amenemhet III, who was king of Upper Egypt and Pharaoh of all Egypt.

Egypt at this time appears to have been a confederation of powerful city-states ruled by lesser kings serving one pharaoh. Cheops was a foreign king of an Egyptian city-state, whose domain reached into the Delta of Egypt.

Hoeh believes the evidence is clear that Cheops must have constructed the Great Pyramid during the beginning of the Israelites' sojourn in Egypt (1726-1487 B.C.) and about the time of the seven years of famine. Hoeh further believes that the noted individual who assisted Cheops was none other than Joseph. History records the man as *Souf*, foreman of the works of Khufu, or as Saf-hotep, one of the twelve brothers (Joseph had eleven brothers) who built the labyrinth of Ancient Egypt for Amenemhet III.

Hoeh further cites a corrupted Egyptian story of the later life of Khufu in which he summons an aged sage to his palace. The sage was said to have lived to the age of 110. Genesis records the death of Joseph at 110 years of age.

It is written in the ancient texts that Cheops/Khufu also wrote a major work of scriptural importance. Manetho, the Egyptian historian, wrote that Cheops was "arrogant toward the gods, but repented and wrote the Sacred Books . . . a work of great importance."

Did the Author of the "Book of Job" Build the Great Pyramid ?

In answering the question of *which* sacred book, Hoeh does a bit of dazzling literary-historical detective work and names Job, author of the Book of Job, as none other than Cheops builder of the Great Pyramid.

How did the central character of one of the most famous religious allegories in all of literature become the king of an ancient Egyptian city-state responsible for an architectural marvel that became one of the seven wonders of the ancient world?

Here, greatly encapsulated, is Hoeh's reasoning:

It seems likely that Cheops' sacred work was not an Egyptian book, since he closed the polytheistic temples and emphasized worship of one god. Cheops was a foreigner, impressing his religion, as well as his politics, upon his Egyptian subjects. They would not be likely to preserve the sacred book of a man whose religious views they would later oppose.

Cheops/Khufu had yet another name, Saaru of Shaaru. Shaaru is another designation for the inhabitants of the region of Mr. Seir. Cheops' domain extended from Mt. Seir to Lower Egypt at the time of Joseph.

A Real-Life "Wizard of Oz"

"Mt. Seir was famous in history as the 'Land of Uz' . . . Uz was a descendant of Seir the Horite (Genesis 36:28)," writes Hoeh. "The Arabs preserve a corruption of Cheops of Mt. Seir or the Land of Uz. They call him the 'wizard of Oz.' "

In Hoeh's opinion, it all adds up:

"Now what individual who dwelled in Uz was arrogant, repented of his sin, and wrote a Sacred Book? None other than Job! And the Sacred Book is the *Book of Job!*"

As an added fillip, Hoeh informs us:

"The ancient Greeks called Job 'Cheops'— pronouncing the letters 'ch' almost as if they were an 'h.' We call Job 'Hiob' in German—and we pronounce the final 'b' as if it were a 'p' much as the Greeks did. Plainly, Cheops is but an altered pronunciation of Job!"

Hoeh offers numerous Bible verses to further substantiate his hypothesis, and concludes that Job/Cheops/Khufu built the Great Pyramid as a monument to "commemorate what Joseph did for Egypt and to mark the border of the territory given to Joseph's family in the land of Egypt by the Pharaoh."

Could the Master Builder Be of a "Different Planet" As Well As a "Different Race"?

While Hoeh builds a good case for his identification of Cheops as the god-tested Job of the Old Testament, one might build an equally good case for the supposition that Cheops might have been an "ancient astronaut" from some extraterrestrial world.

Cheops was said by the Egyptians to have been of a "different race" from them. Perhaps this "difference" might have been much more alien than simply being an Israelite.

Might Cheops have been called a "shepherd because it was deemed that he had come to guide and to comfort the people of his earthly domain?

With his teaching of one god over Egypt's polytheistic hierarchy, did Cheops reveal his higher consciousness?

Perhaps the Sacred Book was a compilation of metaphysical and scientific secrets, the like of which earned him the title of the "wizard of Oz."

And might he have left the pyramid for posterity, not to commemorate any earthly event, but to serve as a beacon light shining through history to alert mankind to the evidence that they are not alone in the universe?

The pyramid may exist as some cosmic educational toy, which serves as an irritant in the mind of modern man as he tries to ponder what appears to be an ancient science, somehow out of context with the nations that surrounded Egypt over 4,000 years ago.

Whether Cheops/Khufu was an ancient astronaut or ancient Israelite, he provided an incredible number of generations with an intriguing and tantalizing mystery of why he constructed such an edifice and for whom.

VII

Mighty Teachers From An Undersea Kingdom

What better place for Atlantis to exist in actuality than under the sea?

Centuries ago, when primitive man asked his mysterious benefactors whence they came, might not the hero-gods have replied: "From beneath the sea in Atlantis." Indeed, the ocean may have named after the undersea kingdom of mighty teachers, who spoke to the intellectually emerging Greeks of the magnificence of their home, Atlantis.

In 1969, Dr. Roger W. Wescott, chairman of the anthropology department at Drew University, Madison, New Jersey, published his *The Divine Animal* (Funk and Wagnalls), in which he presented a serious, well-reasoned theory that UFOnauts landed on earth 10,000 years ago, fully intending to teach *Homo sapiens* a better way of life. When Earth's dominant species demonstrated their innate greed and their penchant for destruction, the extraterrestrial creatures gave up in disgust and withdrew to establish undersea bases.

Although temporarily thwarted in their attempt to build a better world on Earth, the culturally advanced and scientifically superior species may emerge from time to time to conduct certain spot-checks to see if humans have improved. Dr. Wescott theorizes that such monitoring might explain the sightings of UFOs, which have been reported for thousands of years.

The anthropologist also suggests that when the UFOnauts withdrew from Earth's surface, they might have taken some humans along with them to train and to tutor according to their advanced principles. Dr. Wescott conjectures that some of these specially tutored humans might have been returned to the surface where they became leaders.

Some of these trainees worked to change man for good, while others became corrupted by the combination of their secret knowledge and the malleability of the less-advanced surface humans. Wescott said that such individuals as Buddha, Christ, Mohammed, Genghis Khan, and Attila the Hun might have been sent up by the UFOnauts.

Dr. Wescott holds four degrees from Princeton University, which include a bachelor's degree in English and history, a bachelor's degree in general humanities, a master's degree in Oriental studies, and a Doctor of Philosophy degree in linguistics. He has also acquired a Bachelor of Literature degree in social anthropology from Oxford University in England. Dr. Wescott is a Rhodes scholar, a Ford Fellow, and a member of Phi Beta Kappa. Although his *The Divine Animal* does not deal exclusively with the theory of undersea masters, Wescott presents a carefully developed thesis for "Cosmic Tutors" in Chapter Eleven, "Other Creatures, Other Worlds."

"My feeling is that the saucer travelers were pictured as gods by our ancestors," Dr. Wescott was quoted as saying in a press interview. "The saucer creatures began teaching man, but, as man gradually began to master his environment, he also developed to the point where he had material goods and he began to wage wars to obtain the goods he didn't have. It's possible this may have disgusted his Masters so they left."

Cosmic Teachers in Underwater Bases

Dr. Wescott hypothesizes that man's cosmic teachers may have withdrawn from man at this point and established bases under the sea where they could observe man and live comfortably apart from him. "The ocean would have been the easiest place for them to go," he commented. "They could constantly monitor our technology and keep ahead of it."

In Dr. Wescott's opinion, such a theory helps to explain two of the most widespread and persistent legends found among nearly all peoples and all cultures: one, that there was a time when gods walked the earth and tutored man; two, that there was a land called Atlantis, whose thriving civilization met with catastrophe and sank beneath the sea.

Both legends could be distortions of an actual event, which was not a catastrophic annihilation of a continent, but an orderly withdrawal of the "gods," the cosmic teachers, as they transferred their bases from land to the sea floor.

"Since this great relocation," Dr. Wescott said, "saucerites have visited the land only as scouts and observers and never disguised as settlers or leaders."

Dr. Wescott admits that he has no evidence to support his tentative hypothesis, but he noted that several reputable sea captains have seen UFOs going in and out of the ocean, which might indicate that advanced beings have bases there.

"Ezekiel's wheel may have been a flying saucer," Dr. Wescott speculated. "The giants described in Genesis and the angels discussed throughout the Bible may have been these 'Higher Beings.'"

The early Sumerians, the anthropologist said, had legends about giant fishes coming out of the water to teach them. "These so-called fishes may have been manned submarines," he commented.

"When the retrained humans came to the surface, some of them tried to help men, but gave up hope and left as they came, by

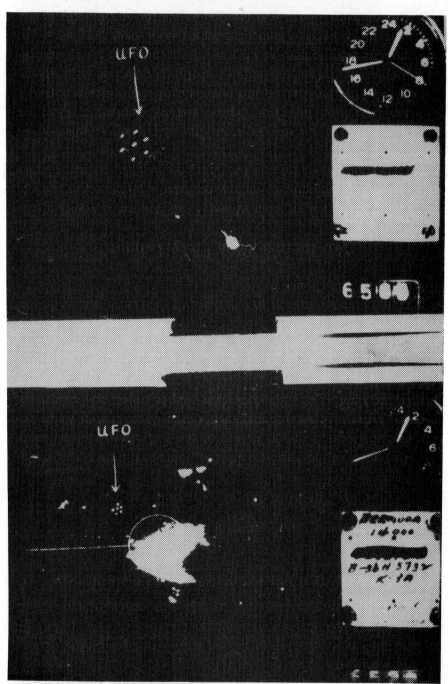

A cluster of UFOs moving across the area of the Atlantic known popularly as the "Bermuda Triangle." These objects were captured on U.S. Air Force radar and the film was placed in Project Bluebook files.

saucer," Dr. Wescott theorized. "This might explain the religious traditions of miraculous ascensions into heaven."

Dr. Wescott ventures an opinion that the extremely man-like forms that have been reported in, or near, stationary UFOs might be the descendants of the human population that the cosmic teachers took with them. The anthropologist cites biblical passages, examples of prehistoric art, and Jewish, Christian, and Islamic traditions, all of which depict manlike creatures appearing from the sky, which early man could only explain by affixing angelic wings to the visiting teachers.

"Rock paintings in the Sahara Desert of North Africa and the Turkestan Steppes of Soviet Asia depict man-like beings with oversized heads, which could be drawings of being wearing space helmets," Dr. Wescott noted.

Dr. Wescott has theorized that the saucer creatures come from a civilization much more advanced than *Homo sapiens*, and may be the most intelligent of hominids. It would appear that these intellectually superior hominids have been visiting our planet longer than our own species has been around.

"These creatures could easily have life-spans of thousands of year," Dr. Wescott was quoted by journalist Harry Edgington. "Remember, the life-span of some life forms here on earth can be measured in minutes. So why couldn't there be other beings who have life-spans many times longer than our own?

"I believe the saucer people would be willing to re-establish contact with us if we could eliminate our own destructiveness. This would open the door to a technology we can only dream of today," Dr. Wescott said.

Gods From the Sea

Was it, we might ask, a whale or an underwater craft of the Cosmic Masters that snatched the drowning Jonah from the turbulent sea and set him back on land and on his way to Nineveh?

The ancient historian Berosus records that the god who gave the Babylonians warning of the coming of the Great Deluge was Chronos, who was associated with a land of plenty in the Atlantic. The Romans called the Atlantic Ocean "Chronium Mare," the Sea of Chronos; and the Pillars of Hercules were also named the Pillars of Chronos by the ancient inhabitants of the Mediterranean. In other words, the master who spoke warnings of coming disaster was identified as a sea god.

Ea, the Chaldean god who brought civilization to the ancestors of the Assyrians, and whose legends are found on the tablets at Nineveh, was represented as half-man and half-fish. Ea was said to have come from a land destroyed by rain and floods, a land now beneath the ocean.

The Indian version of the Deluge tells of Manu, son of Vivasvat, being advised of the coming torrent by a fish that spoke to him from the banks of the Chirini. Later, when Manu and his people construct the great ship that will bear them above the catastrophic flood, the great fish, unwearied, draws them over the waters, bringing the vessel eventually to rest on the highest peak of Himavat.

The Orkney and Hebrides islanders sing of the "Silkies" who dwell in the depth of the sea and occasionally rise up to pass unnoticed on land as humans. According to legend, the Silkies sometimes enter into sexual union with human partners, and some families on the islands pridefully trace their ancestry back to such sea-spawned seed.

It would take a book, rather than a chapter, to delineate all the many myths and legends that tell of gods and enchanted creatures rising up out of the sea to communicate moral lessons, religious dictums, economic truths, or technological insights to astonished human beings on land. The very legends of mermaids and mermen, common to all seafaring people, could in many instances be eye-witness reports from sailors who have glimpsed underwater UFO-nauts peering at them from open submarine hatches.

We need not restrict ourselves to an analysis of ancient myths and folklore. Our contemporary mysteries of the sea contain

A UFO photographed in April, 1967, near Puerto Rico.

innumerable accounts of mysterious unidentified underwater objects cruising our seacoasts and inland waters.

The UFO's apparent affinity for water has long been noted by UFOlogists and flying saucer buffs who chart overflights and landings. Perhaps the UFO enigma might be traced to the inner space of our seas rather than the outer space of our solar system, and the mystery of Atlantis might be solved by seeking Cosmic Masters under the Atlantic rather than turning over rubble and artifacts on Thera.

Strange Mechanical Devices on the Ocean Floor

In 1948, Professor Auguste Piccard brought his unmanned Bathyscaphe up from a record descent of 4,600 feet under the sea from that unknown depth where surface man may never penetrate. Professor Piccard and his crew were so excited by their successful mission, according to J. Y. Cousteau, one of Piccard's associates, that it took them a moment to become cognizant of a very peculiar thing. Although the Bathyscaphe had suffered no actual damage from the intense pressure on the record descent, its aluminum radar mast had been neatly removed, as if a skilled underwater mechanic had accomplished a clean theft.

The American ship *Eltanin*, owned by the Military Sea Transportation Service, was designed for use in the National Science Foundation Antarctic research program. On August 29, 1964, the *Eltanin* was a thousand miles west of Cape Horn, and its crew was busily engaged in photographing the ocean floor, which reached a depth of 13,500 feet in that area. A specially designed camera, housed in a metal cylinder, was being pulled along by a cable.

Later that day when darkroom technicians developed the exposed film, they found that the camera had captured an image of a strange device jutting out of the mud of the ocean. A central mast supported four series of cross rods, which made the object appear to be something like a cross between a television antenna and a telemetry antenna. The cross rods were spaced at ninety-degree angles and showed white knobs on their extremities.

The mysterious object appeared to be man-made and seemed definitely out of place in the anticipated natural environment of the ocean floor. The specially constructed underwater camera had to take pictures at regular intervals. It was only a fortunate, albeit enigmatic, accident that the unidentifiable object had been photographed.

When the *Eltanin* docked at Auckland, New Zealand, on December 4, 1964, a reporter questioned Dr. Thomas Hopkins, senior marine biologist on board, about the 8 x 10 prints of the underwater anomaly. Dr. Hopkins was quoted as saying that the device could hardly be a plant, for at that depth, there was no light. Without light there is no process of photosynthesis and plants cannot live.

Dr. Hopkins was reluctant about declaring the object to be man-made. He estimated the device to be about two feet high and specified its point of discovery as being on the 445,000 mile fault-line rift that encircles the earth.

"If it is some strange coral formation," Dr. Hopkins said, "then no one on board has ever heard of it before. I wouldn't like to say that the thing is man-made, because this brings up the problem of how one would get it there."

Undersea UFOs

Dr. Dmitri Rebikoff, a marine scientist making preparations to explore the Gulf Stream's depths, found himself faced with a similar problem when, on July 5, 1965, he detected and attempted to photograph a fast-moving undersea UFO on the bottom of the warm-water stream that flows from the Florida Keys to Newfoundland and onward to northern Europe. Dr. Rebikoff told Captain L. Jacques Nicholas, project coordinator, that a pear-shaped object, moving at approximately three and one half knots, appeared beneath the various schools of fish.

"At first, from its size, we thought it had to be a shark," Dr. Rebikoff reported. "However, its direction and speed were too consistent. It may have been running on robot pilot. We received no signal from it and therefore we do not know what it was."

On January 12, 1965, according to Issue No. 43 of New Zealand's *Spaceview*, a Captain K_____, an airline pilot on a flight between Whenuapai and Kaitaia, New Zealand, spotted another of the mysterious underwater unidentifiables. He was about one-third of the way across Kaipara Harbor when he saw what he first believed to b a stranded gray-white whale in an estuary. As he veered his DC-3 for a closer look at the object, it became evident to him that he was observing a metallic structure of some sort.

According to *Spaceview*, Captain K_____ noted that the thing was perfectly streamlined and symmetrical in shape . . . had no external control surfaces or protrusions . . . appeared metallic with the suggestion of a hatch on top . . . was resting on the bottom of the estuary and headed toward the south as suggested by the streamlined shape . . . was harbored in no more than 30 feet of water . . . was not shaped like a normal submarine, but approximately 100 feet in length with a diameter of 15 feet at its widest part.

The journal made inquiries of the Navy upon receipt of Captain K_____'s report and learned that it would have been impossible for any known model of submarine to have been in that particular area, due to the configuration of harbor and coastline. The surrounding mud flats and mangrove swamps would make the spot in which Captain K_____ saw his underwater UFO inaccessible to conventional undersea craft.

"Come With Us!"

In the summer of 1969, Englishman John Fairfax rowed his way across the Atlantic, docking in Fort Lauderdale after six harrowing months alone on the ocean.

Reluctantly, Fairfax spoke to the Fort Lauderdale *News and Sun Sentinel* (July 20, 1969) about the most impressive thing that had happened to him during the sea adventure.

"You see," Fairfax said, "I don't believe in those things — never have; but there they were: flying saucers. They could not have been anything else. Venus is the brightest of all the stars, but they were ten times brighter than Venus."

Fairfax explained that there was more involved in the experience than simply observing UFOs. There was a *force*, he told newsmen; it was as though the flying saucers *kept asking him if he wanted to come with them.*

"And I was fighting it and saying back, 'No, no, no,' " Fairfax went on. "It was like telepathy, like being hypnotized. I was hypnotized once, voluntarily. It was like that.

"I had lit a cigarette," he remembered. "Then these luminous saucers swooped down again. There was this magnetic feeling. When they had gone, I realized the cigarette had burned my fingers."

Fairfax could not accept proffered explanations that he might have seen Venus or bright stars. He repeated his statement that the objects were ten times brighter than Venus and said that the UFOs were too bright and too large to be stars or planets and their flight pattern too irregular to have been satellites.

"I don't believe in flying saucers," he said. "But there is nothing else they could be."

A Submerging Saucer in Shag Harbor

On October 3, 1967, the several residents of Shag Harbor, Nova Scotia, were not able to think of any other term than "flying saucers," to describe the 60-foot-long object with a series of bright portholes that they saw glide into the harbor and submerge in the ocean. Within twenty-minutes several constables of the Royal Canadian Mounted Police were on the scene, attempting to reach by boat the spot where about a half mile off shore the sizzling UFO was seen to float and to submerge beneath the surface of Shag Harbor.

A Coast Guard boat and eight fishing vessels joined the constables in time to observe a large patch of yellowish foam and bubbling water. Divers from the Royal Canadian Navy searched the area for two days, but found no physical evidence of any kind. The Halifax *Chronicle-Herald* quoted Squadron Leader Bain of the Royal Canadian Air Force as saying: "We get hundreds of reports every week, but the Shag Harbor incident is one of the few where we may get something concrete on it."

Unidentified Submarine

Captain Julian Lucas Ardanza of the Argentine steamer *Naviero* would have been everlastingly grateful if he might have had the backup support of Royal Canadian constables, navy, and air force on the night of July 30, 1967, when he was some 120 miles off the coast of Brazil. The time was about 6:15 P.M. and the *Naviero* was running at 17 knots. The officers and crew were at their evening meal when Captain Ardanza received a call on the intercom that one of his officers, Jorge Montoya, had spotted something strange near the ship.

According to reports in the Argentine newspapers *La Razon, Cardoba*, and *Los Principios*, Captain Ardanza emerged on deck to behold a cigar-shaped shining object in the sea, not more than fifty feet off the *Naviero's* starboard side. The submarine craft was an estimated 105 to 110 feet long and emitted a powerful blue and white glow. The officers could see no sign of periscope, railing, tower, or superstructure on the noiseless craft. In his twenty years at sea, Captain Ardanza said that he had never seen anything like it.

Chief Office Carlos Lasca ventured that the object was a submersible UFO with its own illumination. The seamen estimated the craft's speed at 25 knots, as opposed to the *Navieros's* 17.

After pacing the Argentine steamer for fifteen minutes, the unidentified submarine object suddenly submerged, passed directly under the *Naviero*, and disappeared into the depths of the ocean, glowing all the while it dove deeper and deeper.

A 200-Foot Cigar-Shaped Object

Just north of the Marianas Islands, some of the deepest areas in the Pacific Ocean, Captain Petore of the *S. S. Morgantown Victory* radioed a message to Anderson Air Force Base, Guam, which reported the sighting of a 200-foot cigar-shaped object on January 13, 1966.

The silent UFO was spotted at an altitude of approximately 400 feet, about one mild starboard beam. The object was visible for three minutes before it hovered starboard quarter and sped away. (From a personal communication to Charles Brown, Editor, *Flying Saucer Review*; May/June 1966).

"An Intense Blue Fiery Tongue"

Chief Mate Torgin Lien of the *T. T. Jawesta*, a vessel of the Norwegian Jahr Shipping Company, reported a UFO on July 8, 1965, while en route from Puerto La Cruz, Venezuela, to the Canary Islands.

According to the report from the ship's log (translated by Gordon Creighton for *Flying Saucer Review*, September/October, 1966): ". . . the lookout on the port side of the bridge reported a bright object in the sky moving in a northerly direction . . . I saw an intense blue fiery tongue which was approaching the sip at tremendous speed . . . I seized binoculars as it passed over the ship . . . at a height of from 200 to 400 metres, under the low clouds. It was bright like a star, and the moonlight was shining through between the low clouds and I could clearly see the outlines of the upper part of it. Its shape was that of a cigar, and I could clearly see a row of square windows and the faint golden-orange colored light from inside it. There was no sign of wings or rudder . . . a little farther back still, behind the body, I could see a tremendous number of globes, and from every globe there was streaming out a blue beam away from the body . . . Its speed was tremendous and it was visible for about 30 to

40 seconds . . . Despite its enormous speed and the closeness of its passage, we could not hear the least sound from it. . . ."

Chief Mate Lien's report was confirmed by a number of the ship's crew, who also witnessed the mysterious UFO.

More Mystery Submarines

On November 14, 1961, Australian and New Zealand warships were conducting naval exercises off Sydney heads when a large unidentified submarine object interrupted their maneuvers. There was no visual sighting of the craft, and the interloper eluded the fleet with speed and ease until contact was lost. The Navy pronounced officially only that it was an "unidentified object."

Early in February, 1960, the Argentine navy, with the assistance of United States experts, alternately depth-bombed and demanded the surrender of submarines thought to be lying at the bottom of Golfo Nuevo, a 40- by 20-mile bay separated from the south Atlantic by a narrow entrance. On a number of occasions, the Argentines had declared that they had the mystery submarine trapped. Once, they announced that they had crippled one of the unidentified subs.

The mysterious submarines (there were at least two) had peculiar characteristics. They were able to function and maneuver in the narrow gulfs for many days without surfacing. They easily outran and hid from surface ships. They were at last able to escape completely, in spite of the combined forces of the Argentine fleet and the most modern U. S. sub-hunting equipment.

Skeptics of the bizarre undersea chase accused the Argentine Navy of timing their dramatic confrontation with mystery submarines with the evaluation of the new navy budget by the Argentine Congress.

On the other hand, UFO buffs enumerated the many reports of strange vehicles seen entering and leaving the sea off the coast of Argentina and pronounced that the unknown objects were underwater spacecraft, rather than terrestrial submarines.

As a third alternative, might we envision an Atlantean Council severely reprimanding two captains of their reconnaissance fleet for allowing themselves to get boxed in and nearly caught by an earthling navy?

A UFO At Omaha Beach

If it is true, as suggested by Dr. Roger W. Wescott, that the cosmic tutors retreated to the sea in disgust after their human students turned to war and slavery, the continued reports of the undersea masters' reconnaissance vehicles must confirm their resolution to remain beneath the ocean.

The seas must certainly have been churning on June 6, 1944, when the Allies invaded Omaha Beach and launched their intensive land campaign against the Nazis in Europe. The day after Normandy had been secured, the U. S. S. *George E. Badger*, a liberty ship, lay anchored in the channel waters off Omaha Beach. Gunner Edward Breckel of Cincinnati was enjoying the aircraft-free sky of a quiet, dreary day, when he spotted a dark, ellipsoidal object about five miles away on the horizon.

Gunner Breckel could see the object was blunted on each end, like a sausage, as it moved in a slow, smooth, circular course about fifteen feet above the surface of the channel.

The craft made absolutely no sound as it moved toward the liberty ship, and it had no protruding parts, as a conventional aircraft would have. Breckel's sharp gunner's eyes told him that it was moving too low and too fast to be a blimp. The UFO remained in view for about three minutes before it disappeared on the horizon.

Again, if we were to imagine the existence of wiser, undersea, hominid cousins, we can visualize the crew of that reconnaissance craft making its grim report of earthling carnage and destruction to a saddened Council of Human Affairs.

Who Are the Unknown Aquanauts?

Whenever one begins to hypothesize about unidentified underwater objects, or UUOs, one cannot help wondering about the true motives of the unknown aquanauts who pilot such craft at such incredible speeds through such depths. Do these aquanauts really have out best interests at heart, as benign cosmic tutors should have, or might they have become somewhat indifferent to struggling, culturally evolving *Homo sapiens*?

If such beings really exist, it would seem unlikely that they are overtly hostile toward man, or we should have been enslaved and conquered long ago. On the other hand, some theorists point out ominously, they may be biding their time until some cosmic time-clock has ticked out an allotted number of hours.

Or, if we have become no more than domesticated, albeit unstable and unreliable, pets in their eyes, might they not have adopted a certain indulgent, but largely indifferent, attitude toward us? A humane motorist tries to avoid hitting a dog running at the side of the road. If, however, the dog should heedlessly dart in front of the automobile or accidentally position itself in a manner where fatal collision would be impossible to avoid, the motorist, while perhaps regretting the incident, will hardly mourn the animal's passing.

Some UFOlogists, who have long been compiling reports of the UUO, felt that such may have been the case when the U.S. nuclear submarine *Thresher* went down in the Atlantic Ocean.

According to official reports, the *Thresher* died through "instantaneous flooding." A sonar listener stated that he had heard a dull thud of considerable impact at great depth. In order to destroy a submarine of such dimensions so quickly that there would be no time for a distress call to the surface, the *Thresher* must have been struck by something large enough to have caused a hole of gigantic proportions.

Again, can we envision our hypothetical Atlantean Council relieving an officer of command for an act of negligence that caused the instantaneous deaths of 129 earthlings?

Our Disappearing Ships

In their September, 1959, issue *Fate* magazine published a list of the U.S. Navy's 18 lost ships, all of which had disappeared under mysterious circumstances in the past 178 years. All but three of the ships on the list disappeared during the nineteenth century, which will mean different things to different researchers (i.e., our improved vessels and navigational equipment have prevented founderings and accidents; our improved vessels and more sophisticated navigation equipment have prevented collisions with unidentified submarine objects).

To examine yet another angle of the strange naval disappearances, if, as has been suggested, the cosmic teachers took a certain number of humans with them when they withdrew to establish their undersea bases, could it be that they, from time to time, gather other representatives of *Homo sapiens* to replace those who die in captivity (perhaps a very lush captivity, but captivity, nonetheless)? There were 2,094 officers, crew, and passengers on those 18 missing vessels.

Disturbingly enough, our improved metal vessels and more sophisticated navigational equipment have certainly not eliminated mysterious underwater rammings of our vessels by unidentified somethings. Whether or not the rammings were accidental, ship owners were left with enormous repair bills, because the guilty party was not thoughtful enough to leave a card with his name and insurance company.

Mysterious Ocean Collisions
with Unidentified Underwater Objects

Ira Pete, owner of the *Ruby E.*, a 67-foot shrimp boat, had his boat sink under mysterious circumstances in the first week in July,

1961. According to Pete, they were fishing in the Gulf of Mexico off Port Arkansas when something hooked into the boat and ripped off its stern. Fortunately for Ira Pete and his two crewmen, there was another fishing vessel close by.

At 3:00 A.M., July 15, 1960, the 24,000-ton Panamanian flag tanker *Alkaid*, with a full cargo of crude oil, was struck by an unidentified submarine object as it passed under the Wiliamsburg Bridge in New York's East River. The collision tore a massive gash in the starboard side of the big ship, forcing the captain to beach her near the United Nations building. Later, the *Alkaid*, on the verge of capsizing, was towed off to a dock.

After two days of Coast Guard hearings and an investigation by the Army Corps of Engineers, whose job it is to keep the harbor waters swept clean, no explanation could be found for the *Alkaid's* mysterious collision with an UUO. Neither could any object be found in the harbor that would have been capable of piercing the tanker's steel hull.

Early in March, 1970, the Danish trawler *SE 140* was fishing northeast of the island of Bronhold in the Baltic when an underwater unidentified started dragging the ship backward. The crewmen told journalists and authorities that the trawler was released only when the trawl wire holding the net broke.

In the fall of 1969, a Swedish trawler, the *Silveroe*, collided with a UUO off the Baltic coast. The Swedish Navy could only offer the weak explanation that the object "could have been a submarine."

On February 5, 1964, the 105-foot yacht *Hattie D.* was rammed by an underwater something near Eureka, California. Ten men and one woman were lifted from the fast-sinking yacht in a dramatic Coast Guard helicopter rescue. The survivors agreed that the *Hattie D.* had been run into by something big made of steel.

Crewman Carl Johnson, when informed that no submarines were reported in the area and that the yacht had sunk in 7,500 feet of water, replied: "I don't care how deep it was there. What holed us was steel and a long piece. There was no give to it at all."

The *Barbara K.* was a steel-hulled, 90-foot vessel owned by the National Marine Terminal of San Diego. On October 31, 1965, about 110 miles south of San Diego with 123 tons of tuna aboard, the *Barbara K.* listed sharply to port, rolled over, and sank in one minute.

Skipper Robert C. Newman said later that he was unaware of hitting any submerged object and that they were not loaded to capacity, yet he only had time to flash an SOS, shout an order to abandon ship, and cut away a small power skiff the vessel was towing. Six of the crewmen clung to debris while the other six climbed into the skiff and headed for another purse seiner, the *Liberty*, four miles away. All hands were saved.

We have already mentioned the Navy's 18 ships, lost since March 18, 1781, and their 2,094 missing officers, crewmen, and passengers. Such a grouping of statistics becomes dwarfed by the grim fact that, **since 1900, more than 1,200 ships of all sizes have been reported missing with all hands and without a trace or clue to their fates.**

The Strange Disappearance of Donald Crowhurst

Earlier in this chapter we noted how John Fairfax reported to newsmen that the UFOs that had appeared above him in the sea had seemed to barrage him with telepathic requests to join them. Fairfax described the experience "like being hypnotized," and mentioned a "magnetic feeling." Perhaps it was such a confrontation that accounted for the disappearance of Donald Crowhurst from his yacht late in 1969.

Crowhurst's *Trimaran* was found abandoned 700 miles southeast of the Azores, 900 miles from his final destination, the English port of Teighmouth. Crowhurst was competing in an around-the world race sponsored by the London *Sunday Times*, and the experienced

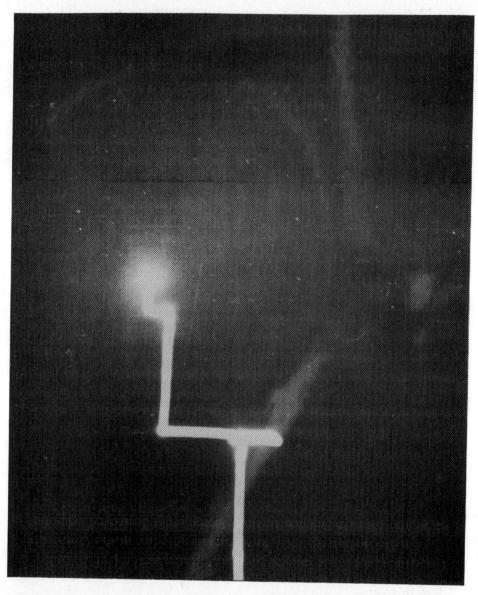

This bright object in the sky caught the attention of a young serviceman home on furlough. He snapped the UFO's picture, then leaving his lens open, caught its subsequent erratic movement. Similar objects with similar flight patterns have been frequently sighted by seamen on the world's oceans.

thirty-six-year-old yachtsman was considered a favorite in the contest. The *Trimaran* was found by a British freighter and bore absolutely no clues to indicate why Crowhurst was not aboard.

Yachting experts conjectured that the *Trimaran* might have been becalmed, encouraging Crowhurst to take advantage of the situation by slipping overboard for a swim. While the yachtsman had paddled about in the ocean, so the explanation went, a small gale may have come up and blown the *Trimaran* out of his reach.

Although the sailing experts' explanation certainly seems a sound one, it can do little to solve the mystery turned up by authorities in London when they discovered that four other small sailing craft had been found abandoned in that same area within less than a month. Weather experts in London said that they had not recorded any weather conditions that could account for the disappearances of the crews, and they testified that no gales had been reported in that part of the ocean.

The ancient Greek legend of the sea sirens and their seductive songs can certainly take on new meaning if one regards them as an Atlantean's hypno-telepathic, "Come with us. Come with us." One might do well to follow Ulysses' example of stuffing the ears with beeswax when planning one's next sailing date.

Vanishing Seamen

On December 18, 1955, in the southwest Pacific, the *Arakarimoa* left Tarawa with her sister ship *Aratoba*. The two vessels were in view of one another until midnight, when the *Arakarimoa* suddenly put on speed and went out of sight.

The *Aratoba* arrived at Tebikerai anchorage at 5:30 A.M. on December 19, but there was no sign of the *Arakarimoa*. The *Arakarimoa's* engines had been recently overhauled and were in excellent running condition. Although port authorities considered engine trouble unlikely, they computed that, with the maximum current drift of about three knots and the direction WNW and WSW, they should have little difficulty locating the missing ship. But why, they wondered, hadn't the *Arakarimoa* radioed for help?

The Royal Colony ship *Nareau* set out at once in search of the *Arakarimoa*. When it returned 36 hours later, it had covered 1,700 square miles without finding a clue to the *Arakarimoa's* fate. According to maximum current drift, an engineless vessel should have drifted no more than 100 miles.

The official explanation was that the *Arakarimoa* had been set upon and completely destroyed by a pirate submarine. Since the ship's only cargo had been 700 empty copra sacks, robbery seemed a weak motive; but at the time, it was as good an official explanation as any.

On February 3, a Royal New Zealand Air Force Sunderland searched for a maverick sub that had been sighted near Kandavu in Fijian waters by the captain and crew of the Komaiwai.

Although the Air Force was unable to locate the submarine, several passengers aboard the *Tuivalvala* saw a metallic object in the waters between Kandavu and Benqua Islands. The UUO lay between the passengers and the sun and was seen to have no mast, but "something like a conning tower." It disappeared suddenly below the surface of the water, faster, it seemed, than a conventional submarine might manage the business of submerging.

In February, 1948, a frenzied SOS was transmitted by the Dutch vessel *S. S. Ourang Medan*. The radio call told of death coming to the captain, the whole crew. After a series of jumbled dots and dashes, the message ended tersely with: "I die."

Rescue ships from Dutch Sumatra and British Malaya rushed to the location of the ship in distress and found her only a few miles from the position broadcast.

Investigating parties were met by a grotesque sight. The dead officers were sprawled in the wheelhouse, chartroom, and wardroom. Dead crew members lay everywhere: on their bunks, in the passageways, on the decks. The wireless operator sat slumped at his post in the radio shack, his lifeless hand still on the sending key.

On each of the dead men's faces was a look of convulsive horror. When the corpses wee examined more closely in an attempt to determine the cause of death, medical personnel could find no sign of injuries or symptoms of disease on any of the bodies. The men all looked as though they had been literally frightened to death.

As the rescue ship prepared to tow the blighted vessel into port, flames suddenly belched forth from Number 4 hold. Within moments the fire was so widespread that the boarding party was forced to hastily abandon the ship and return to the safety of their own vessels. In an incredibly short time, the *S. S. Ourang Medan* seemed to leap into the air in her death agony, as a violent explosion racked her metal frame. The ill-fated ship slowly slid beneath the waters, burying any clue to the fate of her officers and crew in the depths of the sea.

Powerful Electromagnetic Disturbances

On October 24, 1965, the auxiliary sloop *Vision 4* was cruising off Milford, Connecticut, skippered by Alfred Stanford, a retired U. S. Navy captain. Aboard as Stanford's guest was the noted Labrador explorer Dr. Paul Sheldon, holder of the Cruising Club's Blue Water Medal.   The sloop was about four miles off Charles Island, steering for the harbor entrance from out in Long Island Sound, when the compass suddenly began a strange, clockwise circling. The engine was running slowly, about 1,000 rpm, and there was no excessive amount of vibration; yet the compass continued its clockwise circling for about ten minutes, or three-quarters of a mile, before it steadied.

Captain Stanford later noted that he had the compass on the *Vision 4* adjusted for zero error by the experienced navigator, and he commented that the compass had been free of error during a full intensive season of cruising.

Such erratic behavior on the part of the sloop's compass suggests a very powerful electromagnetic field beneath the surface of the costal waters over which *Vision 4* was cruising. Captain Stanford told newsmen that the peculiar rotation of his compass could not have come from the sloop's engine, because he had a disconnect switch on the generator field coil, which he had pulled without effect. There had to have been a submerged *something* beneath his sloop, Captain Stanford said, that had been playing havoc with his compass.

There is a great deal of evidence to indicate that magnetic fields can affect the human brain and produce hallucinations, speech changes, and general confusion and disorientation. Not only might an electromagnetic field make a compass needle go berserk, but such a field might very well befuddle seasoned pilots into hysteria and confuse hapless fishermen and yachtsmen into jumping overboard in their mental distress.

Strange Undersea Craft

Two New Zealand commercial fishermen, R. D. Hanning, skipper of the *Eleoneai*, and W. J. Johnson, may have had a glimpse of such a mysterious mechanical *something* and were left both frightened and shaken by the experience.

The strange undersea craft broke surface when the *Eleoneai* was just off New Zealand's Rugged Islands. The fishermen described the UUO as having had a tapered structure which rose about fifteen feet above the surface. They estimated that it measured about five feet high at the top and twelve feet at the waterline. They saw no sign of a periscope or a railing, but they did notice a peculiar box-shaped object about ten feet long and five feet high that surfaced about thirty feet away from the larger craft.

Later, at the interview with naval officers who had learned of the sighting, Skipper Hanning expressed his umbrage at the suggestion that the two well-seasoned seamen could mistake whales, logs, or floating debris for a mechanical craft.

What Is "Swallowing" Tugboats, Yachts and Their Crews?

On January 11, 1967, a four-year-old tugboat, the *Gulf Master*, and her five crewmen disappeared off Sechelt, British Columbia.

There had been no more reason for this 66-foot tugboat to have vanished than there had been for the tug that had disappeared in the same area less than a month before. The only clue that investigators had to go on was the reports of extensive UFO activity above the water in that area, both before and after the disappearance of the two tugboats. The Marine Services Division of the Department of Transport chose not to pursue a correlation between the sightings of the UFOs and the vanishing tugboats.

Men have been disappearing along with their ships since the first primitive seafarer set out from shore astride a log. The fact that such things have been occurring since the dawn of civilization, however, offers scant consolation to the families of those whose loved ones have disappeared under mysterious circumstances in these days of radio, radar, and instant aerial search parties.

At 9:00 P.M. on December 24, 1967, the 23-foot inboard-outboard *Witchcraft* radioed a distress signal from a position about one mile east of Miami. The Coast Guard said later that it had been on the scene within 20 minutes but that they had been unable to find any trace of the luxury boat. Both the Coast Guard and the Civil Air Patrol spent a full day searching for the craft without success.

It becomes difficult to accept such mysteries of the sea as stoically as our ancestors once received news of similar unexplained disappearances of ships and their crews. The notion that a 23-foot craft could completely disappear almost within sight of a large city and within 20 minutes of the Coast Guard's arrival penetrates the brain with icy shards.

It requires a rather lively imagination to envision a gigantic sea monster rising out of the brine to swallow a 23-foot inboard-outboard whole before an efficient and conscientious Coast Guard can come to the rescue.

On the other hand, there may be undreamed of and unknown *mechanical* monsters capable of "swallowing" a 23-foot craft without the least indigestion.

"Boiling" Sea Water and Earth Tremors

Early in 1968, UFO researchers were receiving reports from commercial fishermen who were complaining of flying saucers entering and leaving the water and of areas in the Gulf of Mexico where the ocean was "boiling" in circles.

We are conditioned to consider that water can only boil when something is producing a requisite amount of heat. It is difficult to avoid wondering just what an unidentified someone is "cooking up" for us in those areas of boiling, turbulent waters. And one can hardly resist making a mental association between boiling sea water and such undersea erratics as the one the *Eltanin* photographed on our planet's 45,000 mile fault line.

Could those oft-sighted underwater unidentified objects and such mysterious "machines" on Earth's fault lines be responsible for such unusual weather and seismic disturbances as the following:

The Pacific Ocean is becoming warmer. One scientist reports that over the 200,000 square miles of the California current region alone this warming represents the equivalent in energy of 560 billions barrels of fuel—nearly the world's total resources. The sun would have to deliver four times the amount of heat actually received by Earth to warm this volume of water. Scientists cannot determine the source of this heat.

The island of Dominica in the British West Indies has been shaken by mysterious earth tremors which geophysicists have not been able to explain. Seismologists from University College in Trinidad reported the tremors to be quite unlike those produced by earthquakes or explosions. Although Dominica is a volcanic island, there have been no eruptions in recorded time.

On December 26, 1967, the University of California's seismic instruments recorded two earthquakes for Vancouver Island, only to have authorities at Victoria deny any quakes in their area. (Did the instruments malfunction, or was there other quake-like activity beneath the sea?)

On December 12, 1967, there were sudden underwater volcanic eruptions in the Tonga Trench, 2,900 miles south-south-west of Hawaii.

On January 15, 1968, within a few hours,

hurricane winds lashed the Scottish coast;

a sudden thaw in normally winter-frigid Austria caused flash floods;

a sudden rise in temperature from record lows sent winter-conditioned Scandinavia into chaos;

violent gales broke all wind records in England and claimed lives throughout the British Isles;

a foot of snow fell on Jerusalem, while outside the city, sand-storms whipped the desert areas.

On July 5, 1970, the Chicago *Sun-Times* carried a United Press International release which told of a U.S. space agency report of a "cavity" in the ocean. NASA stated that it was using a ship-satellite technique to measure a "curious depression" in the sea surface over the Atlantic's deepest hole.

According to UPI: "The depression, dipping as much as 80 feet below normal sea level, is directly over the Puerto Rico trench . . . Scientists attribute the 'cavity' in the ocean surface to *an unusual distribution of mass beneath the ocean floor*. This causes deflection of the pull of gravity, which ordinarily is vertical." (Italics are the author's.)

Unknown Footprints on the Sea Bed

Whether they be cosmic tutors or other forms of alien or native intelligence, some unknown agencies seem to know their way very well along the bottom of our sea beds. What is more, someone, or something, has been leaving tracks.

In 1958, Columbia University scientists photographed something that looked remarkably like chicken tracks 7,000 below the Arctic ice. What they were, how they got there, and how long they had been there before the camera pictured them remains a mystery.

In that same year, Dr. A. Laughton of the National Institute of Oceanography told the British Association for the Advancement of Science at a meeting in Dublin that he had photographed mysterious footprints with a camera lowered nearly three miles down to the bed of the Atlantic Ocean.

"It would be interesting to know what makes them," he said of the tracks. "We have studied the pictures closely for evidence of something at the end of these tracks. So far, we have not found it."

During the International Geophysical Year, a story leaked to the popular press that the Columbia University scientists had also photographed giant humanoid footprints marring the otherwise smooth layer of ocean floor silt. The New York *Herald Tribune*, with tongue firmly in cheek, suggested that the Abominable Snowman had a submarine brother. Pressured for some kind of answer that would be deemed acceptable to scientific orthodoxy, the scientists credited the footprints to mudworms that had curled up in the shape of large human footprints and spaced themselves equidistantly.

It is difficult to champion the cause of pseudo-footprints that may have been made by unconsciously artistic mudworms. We should like to hear from individuals who claim to have seen the persons who may have been responsible for making such footprints.

The Siren Song of Atlanteans

At dawn on January 29, 1921, a Coast Guard boat at Hatteras Inlet, North Carolina, approached the grounded *Carroll J. Deering*. When the crew boarded the vessel, they found her deserted except for a cat. There was food in the cooking pots and the plates had been set for mess, but there was not a single soul aboard ship.

In a subsequent investigation, a member of a lighthouse crew some 60 miles south of Ocracoke reported that Captain William B. Wormell had hailed the lighthouse the day before the *Deering* had grounded. Captain Wormell had asked that a tug be sent from Norfolk to tow them to port because a storm had torn away the

Deering's anchors. The lighthouse crewman stated that he had seen *small, brownish-skinned men* among the regular seamen.

When the crewman went to the radio to call Norfolk, he was puzzled to find that his equipment was inoperable. He left the lighthouse in time to hail a nearby southbound steamer and ask it to relay the *Deering's* call for assistance. The steamer ignored the man's request, suddenly changed its course, and lowered a tarpaulin to hide its name from the lighthouse crew.

There may be a clue of sorts in this whole eerie business of the *Carroll J. Deering.* Our smallish, reddish-brown-skinned Atlanteans with their siren's song of invitation to come with them to their undersea paradise may already have lulled and controlled the crew of the *Deering.* They may even have boarded the vessel after the storm with promises of assistance.

The inexplicable failure of the radio to work when the lighthouse crewman went to relay Captain Wormell's message may indicate that the captain was not completely under their hypnotic spell and steps had to be taken to blank out the lighthouse radio. Indeed, Captain Wormell's daughter later made the discovery that the entries for the last six days in the ship's log had been made in a hand other than her father's and in a script that did not appear to match the handwriting of any crewman.

The sudden appearance of a steamer and its subsequent bizarre behavior seems to indicate that it was something other than what it had at first appeared to be.

As long as we are theorizing in this vein, we may as well suggest that the outer shell of a conventional steamer may well have hidden a sleek and powerful submarine craft.

We must admit, of course, that the only facts in this case are the rotting hulk of the *Deering* on Ocracoke Island and the complete disappearance of Captain Wormell and his crewmen within minutes or hours after they left the lighthouse. Other less imaginative theorists might favor midget Mexican pirates as the true culprits.

On December 18, 1967, an early morning fire at the University of Miami Marine Science Institute completely destroyed one-of-a-kind papers that were the product of seventeen years of marine research and which had involved nearly ten million dollars in scientific work. The fire struck the Institute shortly before 2:00 A.M. and was out of control in an hour, as the flames fed upon the accumulated, irreplaceable scientific paperwork.

Although it may be considered a rather outré speculation, could it be possible that an unidentified, unknown *someone* might have been aware of some clue to fantastic underwater cities and submarine bases that lay hidden among the paperwork and photographs?

Could an unknown undersea council have decreed that the piecing together of certain still ambiguous research items would have given the scientific establishment of *Homo sapiens* too-much, too-soon knowledge and ordered the Institute put to the torch?

As it stands now, unless a Bathysphere takes a reel of film of one of these secretive submarines or snaps a photograph of a crew of hominid divers, we shall be asked to believe that our commercial fishermen, our military and commercial sea and air crews, and our coastal residents are seeing nothing but "seaweed gas."

VIII

Masters Of The Inner-Earth Empire

A hundred years before William Reed wrote *The Phantom of the Poles* ("scientific evidence proving that the earth is hollow") and Marshall B. Gardner privately published his *A Journey to the Earth's Interior* and when Jules Verne, who would later write *A Journey to the Center of the Earth*, was only nine years old, Edgar Allan Poe published his longest tale, "The Narrative of Arthur Gordon Pym," which told of a fantastic land located in Earth's center, reached by a hole at the pole. So convincingly did Poe weave the pseudoscientific beginning of his narrative that Horace Greeley soberly endorsed the Pym adventure as a true account, without finishing the tale and encountering its later sections of obvious fantasy.

In 1823, Captain John Cleve Symmes, a dour, humorless, retired war hero, petitioned the U. S. Congress for funds to conduct an expedition to explore the hollow earth. Captain Symmes and his small band of followers felt somewhat anointed for the task because the great American clergyman Cotton Mather had defended the theory of a hollow earth in his book *The Christian Philosopher*. Mather, in turn, had developed his hypothesis from a little-known essay penned by English astronomer Edmund Halley in 1692.

Quaint notions from an unsophisticated and romantic past, smiles the modern reader. Lest he remain secure in such an appraisal, he should be informed that one of the greatest military-scientific aggregations of this century was also prepared to explore and to exploit the alleged world within our planet.

The Third Reich and the
Quest for the Hollow Earth

In April, 1942, Nazi Germany sent out an expedition composed of its most visionary scientists to seek a military vantage point in the "Hollow Earth." Although the safari of leading scientists left at a time when the Third Reich was putting maximum effort in their drive against the Allies, Goering, Himmler, and Hitler enthusiastically endorsed the project.

The Fuehrer had long been convinced that Earth was concave and that man lived on the *inside* of the globe. According to theory advanced by the Nazi scientists, if the Third Reich were to position their most astute radar experts in the proper geometric area, they would be able to determine the position of the British Fleet and the Allied bomber squadrons, because the concave curvature of the globe would enable infrared rays to accomplish long-distance monitoring.

When the Nazi exponents of the Hollow Earth hypothesis sent the expedition to the island of Rugen, they had complete confidence in their pseudo-scientific vision. Those nearest the Fuehrer shared his belief that such a *coup* as discovering the entrance to the Inner World would convince the Masters who lived there that the Nazis were truly deserving of mixing their blood in the hybridization of a master race.

An important element in the Nazi mythos was the belief that representatives of a powerful, underground secret race emerged from time to time to walk among *Homo sapiens*. Hitler's frenzied desire to breed a select race of Nordic types was inspired by his obsessive hope that it should be the Germanic peoples who would be chosen above all other humans to interbreed with the subterranean supermen in the mutation of a new race of heroes, demigods, and god-men.

DR. C.L. BURDICK.

As amazing at it may seem, footprints such as these, which appear definitely to be human, have been discovered in geological strata indicative of 250 million years old. The largest number in recent years have been discovered in the Southwestern states of Utah, Nevada, Oklahoma, and Texas.

Authors Louis Pauwels and Jacques Bergier quote Hermann Rauschning, governor of Danzig during the Third Reich, who repeated a conversation he had once had with Hitler concerning the Fuehrer's plan to assist nature in developing mutants.

"The new man is living amongst us now!" the dictator said emphatically. "He is here! Isn't that enough for you? I will tell you a secret. I have seen the new man. He is intrepid and cruel. I was afraid of him."

Rauschning stated that Hitler seemed to be in a kind of ecstasy as he spoke those words.

According to persistent rumors, there exists evidence to indicate that Hitler may have been mediumistic. Indeed, Hitler's birthplace, the little Austrian village of Branau-on-the-Inn, has long been a center of spiritualism in Europe, and it has been said that the infant Adolf shared the same wet-nurse with Willy Schneider, who along with his brother Rudi, became a world famous medium.

Legends of the Old Ones

There are persistent legends in nearly every culture that tell of the Old Ones, an ancient race who populated the earth millions of years ago. The Old Ones, an immensely intelligent and scientifically advanced race, have chosen to structure their own environment under the surface of the planet and manufacture all their necessities.

The Old Ones are hominid, extremely long-lived, and pre-date *Homo sapiens* by more than a million years. The Old Ones generally remain aloof from the surface peoples, but from time to time, they have been known to offer constructive criticism; and it has been said, they often kidnap human children to tutor and rear as their own. There is scarcely a culture known to man that does not have at least one segment of their folklore built around troll-like creatures that live underground and do their best to steal the children of surface folk.

In virtually all the legends, the Old Ones have gone underground to escape natural catastrophes or the hidden death that exists in the life-giving rays of our sun. At this point a persistently propagated theory of Atlantis crosses the path of the Old Ones, the mysterious Teachers from the Caves, which declares that those Atlanteans who survived the great cataclysm learned to perpetuate themselves in underground caverns.

This version of the destruction of the fabled continent has Atlantis shattering into the ocean as the result of a tremendous nuclear blast ignited by a self-destructive super science. The necessity for finding underground accommodations is thus compounded by the deadly radiation on the surface of the earth and by the knowledge that an existence away from the normal radioactivity of the sun is a healthier one.

The nemesis of radioactive fallout is, of course, a comparatively recent addition to the legend, but the explosion of our own nuclear devices set off minuscule mushroom clouds in the brains of thousands of Atlantean buffs, who felt that they had at last been given the key to the reason why the continent got lost in the first place: Atlantis had been a nation of super scientists, who blew their continent and themselves to bits. Then, when UFOs began to be sighted in 1947, an association between the underground survivors of a technically superior race and the flying saucers became obvious to them: the Atlanteans were emerging from their subsurface kingdom to warn their suddenly dangerous surface successors that nuclear power had the potential to destroy civilization.

Underworld Supermen

An alternate theory, very close to the one set forth by Dr. Roger Wescott concerning undersea cosmic tutors, has it that the Cave Masters are surviving colonies of spacemen, who after walking the earth in god-like mien, grew disgusted with *Homo sapiens* and retreated to underearth bases from which they might watch over the primitive species' intellectual and cultural development. The Buddhists have even incorporated *Agharta*, a subterranean empire, into their theology and fervently believe in its existence and in the reality of underworld supermen, who periodically surface to oversee the progress of the human race.

Among the Amerindians, the Navajo legends teach that the fore-runners of man came from beneath the earth. The ancient ones were possessed of supernatural powers and were driven from their caverns by a great flood (yet another echo of the traditional Atlantis myth). Once on the surface, they passed along great knowledge to humans before they once again sought secret sanctuary.

The Pueblo Indians' mythology places their gods' place of origin as being an inner world connected to the surface people by a hole in the north. Mesewa, according to the Pueblos, was succeeded as leader of the gods by his brother, Oyoyewa, which some researchers have pointed out is quite similar to the Hebrew Yahweh.

The Hollow Earth

For several years then, in one camp or another, Atlantis has been associated with the Hollow Earth mythos:

(1) An ancient hominid race antedating *Homo sapiens* by a million years withdrew from the surface world and this physical withdrawal gave birth to the legend of Atlantis;

(2) Atlantis, an actual prehistoric world of super science, blew itself to bits and its survivors sought refuge from radioactivity under the crust of the earth;

(3) Extraterrestrial hominids planted a colony on Earth, gave intellectually inferior *Homo sapiens* a boost up the evolutionary ladder, then grew aghast at man's perpetual barbarism and withdrew to a more aloof position underground, thereby giving rise to the legend of Atlantis as a lost culture.

Dr. Raymond Bernard's *The Hollow Earth*, originally published by Fieldcrest Publishing Company of New York, has become the classic work in the rather amorphous field of "proving" the existence of an Inner Earth. In his introduction to the book, Dr. Bernard promises to prove that ". . . the earth is hollow and not a solid

sphere . . . and that its hollow interior communicates with the surface
by two polar openings. . . ."

Dr. Bernard's *magnum opus* discloses that Rear Admiral Richard
E. Byrd flew *beyond* rather than *over* the North Pole and that his
later expedition to the South Pole passed 2,300 miles *beyond* it.
According to Dr. Bernard, the North and South Poles have never
been reached, because they do not exist. In his view, the nation
whose explorers first find the entrance to the hollow interior of the
earth will become the greatest nation in the world.

There is no doubt, the reader learns, that ". . . the mysterious
flying saucers come from an advanced civilization in the hollow
interior of the earth . . . that, in event of nuclear world war, the
hollow interior of the earth will . . . provide an ideal refuge for the
evacuation of survivors of the catastrophe. . . ."

The Shaver Mystery of "Deros" and "Teros"

In the March, 1945 issue of *Amazing Stories* Editor Ray Palmer
introduced the Shaver Mystery, a purported "racial memory" of a
young welder named Richard Shaver, who first claimed to have
remembered a life in the caves, then, later, maintained that he had
recently been in the vast underground civilization of cave-dwellers.
Life magazine (May 21, 1951) called the Shaver Mystery ". . . the
most celebrated rumpus that ever racked the science fiction world."
Richard Shaver, however, has never called his accounts anything
other than factual reportage.

It is Richard Shaver's contention that in prehistoric times, when
our solar system was young, Earth was inhabited by a race of cosmic
super-beings who had come here from another solar system.
Although the Elder Race were not truly immortals, they had
discovered secrets of incredible longevity. This, together with their
highly developed scientific technology, caused them to be regarded
as gods by the primitive and unsophisticated humans. The Elder
Race possessed fantastic mechanical devices, which Shaver calls
"mech," capable of projecting three-dimensional images, scanning

over great distances, curing diseases, producing food and clothing, and killing and destroying life when necessary.

After a time the Elder Race, the Titans, began to notice that the once beneficent sun now contained detrimental rays which were shortening their life-span by causing premature aging. To escape the harmful rays of the sun, the Elder Race entered deep underground caverns and began carving a fantastic subterranean kingdom, using their ray guns to disintegrate rock. Soon they had constructed powerful machines which could duplicate the health-giving rays of the sun while excluding the detrimental radioactivity.

Homo sapiens continued to evolve in the sun, ignorant of the rays which shortened his life-span, and puzzled by the withdrawal of his gods. However, Shaver tells his readers, the Elder Race was not without its sensualists, and certain of its members, particularly the lesser ones, varied greatly in morality and intelligence.

Perhaps the majority of the Elder Race regarded their lesser evolved human cousins with the superiority and ill-concealed contempt that a pompous research scientist might feel walking amongst stone age aborigines. Others may have exploited the females of *Homo sapiens* and may even have set the barbaric tribes against each other for the perverse pleasure of the Elder Race, who may have openly rooted for, and secretly assisted, their favorite tribes and warriors. The more humane among the Elder Race did their best to assist the primitive humans to develop a more functional culture and technology. According to Shaver, the ancient myths and legends are the unsophisticated surface dwellers' version of the myriad activities of the Elder Race.

After a time, the Shaver Mystery has it, the Elder Race became dissatisfied with life on Earth. Spaceships were sent to find another more suitable world where they could live on the surface without fearing negative rays from the sun. When the scouts returned with word of a planet with a beneficial sun, a mass exodus was at once set in motion.

Because of the great distance involved and the limited number of spacecraft large enough to serve as transports, the vast majority of their marvelous machines of super science were sealed in underground caverns. Desperate experimentation with the "mech" brought about certain radiations that destroyed a portion of the brain of many of the underpeople and produced a dangerous form of hereditary insanity.

Vast numbers of the cave people began to degenerate into physically stunned near-idiots, incapable of constructive reasoning. Shaver tells his readers that these are the "dero," detrimental — or degenerate — robots. "Robot" as Shaver used the word does not mean a mechanical representation of man, but is rather a designation for those who are controlled, or obsessed, by degenerative forces.

The deros, due to their hereditary brain damage, are completely devoid of any moral sense or humane instinct. They do harm at every opportunity and they gain immense satisfaction from the sufferings of others. They have mastered the use of certain of the "mech," and they direct negative rays at the surface dwellers whenever possible.

Their greatest delight comes in luring, or kidnapping, humans into the caverns and debasing them in sadistic orgies, which usually result in death or enslavement for the unfortunate captive. According to Shaver, the details of some of these grotesque debaucheries reached the surface world and established the foundations for the accounts of devils, demons, and the underworld hells of religion.

Standing between the degenerate dero and the complete annihilation of the surface people are the "tero" (The Elder RAce used T as a symbol of their religious philosophy, so the "t" in tero stands for good). The tero have devised a means of staving off many of the degenerative effects of their poisonous partial science by use of machines and chemicals and the direction of beneficial rays.

Through centuries of experimentation, the tero have nearly mastered manipulation of the "mech" left by the leaders who deserted their ancestors. They are able to defend themselves from the dero and are able to keep the dero from swarming up to the surface world *en masse*.

Although many of the tero harbor friendly sentiments toward their human cousins above the caverns, they still consider man too barbaric to be entrusted with the secrets of the "mech."

In ancient times, an extensive trade and exchange was carried on between the tero and the surface peoples, but as humans became more sophisticated and their communications became more efficient, the tero have almost completely withdrawn from open intercourse with the surface world. This surviving remnant of the Elder Race is determined to keep its Inner World a secret from the humans until man has matured enough to share the marvels of the "mech," still operable after millions of years.

"A Warning to Future Man"

Richard Shaver originally entitled his initial short story, "A Warning to Future Man," because, according to his observations during his alleged sojourn in the caves, the dero are becoming more numerous and have begun to weaken the more pacifistic tero with their constant attacks. The greatest danger lies in the uncomfortable fact that the dero also have access to the "mech" of Elder Race's super science, but they do not have the requisite intelligence or the highly developed moral sense needed to handle the machines responsibly.

Both the tero and the dero have learned to master vision ray machines that can penetrate rock and view scenes all over the earth; teleportation units that can effect instant transport from one point to another; bizarre "mech" that can create "solid" illusions, dreams, compulsions; the aerial craft humans refer to as "flying saucers"; death rays; "stim" machines to revitalize the reproductive organs (remember the deros' penchant for orgies); "ben" rays that heal and restore the body. Because these fantastic products of technology as yet unequaled on Earth are still in perfect working order due to the high degree of scientific craftmanship with which they were constructed, it is quite easy to see how the remnants of the Elder Race could still appear god-like even in our nuclear age. Shaver maintains

Author-Editor Ray Palmer. Did he create the Shaver Mystery to boost sales of *Amazing Stories*? Or did the tales actually reveal the mind-boggling details of an Inner Earth Empire of Monsters and Masters?

that the dero, little more than sadistic idiots, have taken enormous delight in precipitating our wars, arranging terrible accidents, and even in creating nightmares, as they train "dream mech" on unsuspecting humans as they sleep.

Editor Ray Palmer claimed that the issue of *Amazing Stories* (March, 1945) that carried the first Shaver fact-fiction piece brought in an unprecedented mail response of 50,000 letters, all of which Palmer said ". . . stated that Shaver spoke the truth, there actually were caves, and dero, and rays, and stim, and contrived train wrecks, and mental control, and thought records, and Titans, and ancient spaceships, and radioactive death raining down on us from the sun."

Ray Palmer kept the mystery and the controversy going for four years, in more than fifty consecutive issues of *Amazing Stories, Fantastic Adventures, Mammoth Adventures*, and even *South Sea Stories*. The furor the Shaver Mystery set off among the science fiction and Fortean buffs continues to break out in periodic brush fires. Richard Shaver continues to contribute his "memories" to mimeographed fanzines, and occasionally, to the late Ray Palmer's *Search* magazine, published in Amherst, Wisconsin.

Both Shaver and Palmer were put on the defensive and were continually being asked to answer charges that the clever and talented Palmer did not simply prefabricate the whole Inner Earth mystery himself, permitting an ingenious Shaver to front for the circulation-building hoax.

Before his death, Palmer told me: "Although I added all the trimmings, I did not alter the factual basis of Mr. Shaver's manuscript except in one instance. Here, perhaps, I made a grave mistake. However, I could not bring myself to believe that Mr. Shaver had actually gotten his alphabet and his 'Warning to Future Man,' and all the 'science' he propounded from actual underground people. Instead, I translated his thought-records into 'racial memory' and felt sure this would be more believable to my readers, and after all, if this were all actually based on fact, a reasonable and perhaps actual explanation of what was going on in Mr. Shaver's mind—which is where I felt it really was going on, and not in any caves or via any telaud rays or telesolidograph projections of illusions from the cavern ray operators."

Strange Tales of Underground Dwellers

Timothy Green Beckley, editor of *Innerlight* newsletter, has probably published more material on Richard Shaver and his cave dwellers than any other writer-editor outside of Ray Palmer. Beckley tells of finding a record of ostensible dero activity *Black Range Tales*, a book published by James A. McKenna in 1936.

McKenna, who purports to be writing a factual account, tells of observing two Indian maids walk *into* the wall of a canyon, then reappear with buckets of water for their burros.

After the girls had left, McKenna and a friend, Cousin Jack, investigated and found the entrance to a carefully hidden cave, which sheltered an underground spring.

Later that night, Cousin Jack awoke screaming in pain, complaining of someone sticking him with needles. The two men were puzzled to discover that some form of electricity seemed to be present in the canyon and that the current had run through the grass and caused the sensation of needles being pricked into flesh.

At dawn, according to McKenna, the two men resolved to explore the strange cave. They had not penetrated very far into its depth, however, before they retreated, sickened by a sulphuric odor, shocked by the sound of a moaning voice crying for "mercy," and startled by a find of several human skeletons.

Fortean researcher Ronald Calais found an account dating from 1770 which relates the experience of a laborer in Staffordshire, England, who while engaged in digging a tunnel, claimed to have heard the rumble of heavy machinery coming from behind a large, flat stone.

Prying the rock aside with his pick, the laborer was amazed to discover a stone stairway that led deep into the ground. Certain that he had come upon some ancient tomb, the man started down the steps with visions of buried treasure filling his brain.

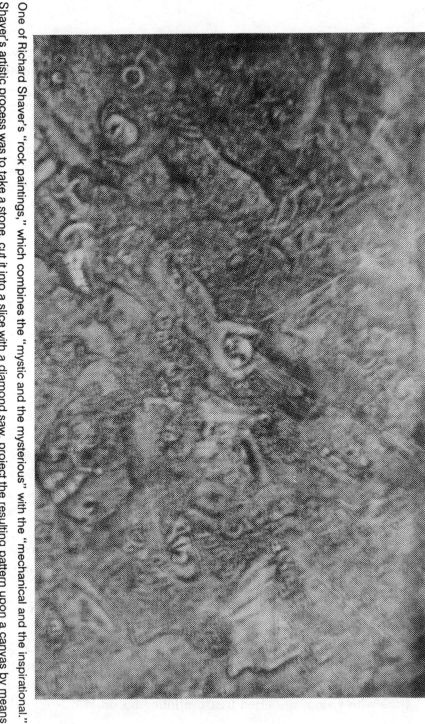

One of Richard Shaver's "rock paintings," which combines the "mystic and the mysterious" with the "mechanical and the inspirational." Shaver's artistic process was to take a stone, cut it into a slice with a diamond saw, project the resulting pattern upon a canvas by means of an opaque projector, then spray the canvas with various combinations of paints and inks.

Instead, the man swore, he found himself in a large stone chamber with the sounds of machinery becoming louder and a hooded figure fast approaching him with a baton-like object in a raised hand. The terrified laborer fled back up the stone stairway to the safety of the surface world.

By way of comparison, Calais couples this account with the comments of David Fellin and Henry Throne, who survived a 1963 Pennsylvania mine cave-in. The two miners claimed that they saw a huge door open to reveal beautiful marble steps with men clothed in "weird outfits" staring at them. The men were certain they had experienced reality, rather than hallucinations.

Monsters in Mining Tunnels

Tough Irish laborers insisted that it was not hallucination haunting them in a 40-yard stretch of tunnel that was cut under the Thames River in London in the all of 1968.

Big Lou Chalmers felt something brush his neck. When he turned around, he saw something in the shape of a man with his arms stretched out. "I didn't stop to make out details," he said later. "I just ran."

A fellow named Nobby saw the figure and came up from the tunnel "as white as a sheet." He went for a stiff drink, quit his job, and never came near the tunnel again.

John Daley told journalists that the figure wore a brown overcoat and a cap.

"We've heard a lot about people being buried down there who died in the plague centuries ago," the laborer said. "But that wouldn't account for the fellow wearing modern dress."

Alfred Scadding was the sole survivor of the famous 1936 Moose River Mine disaster. Minutes before the mines caved in, he was on his way to join other workers.

"I came to a cross cut, a tunnel running across the one I was in, and as I passed I looked left," he said later. "I saw a small light, like a flashlight, about two feet from the ground and swinging as if in someone's hand, moving away from me. I have an absolutely clear and detailed memory of that incident."

Scadding was told, after his rescue, that no human being was down in the mine at that time other than the two men who were trapped with him. "Two minutes after I saw that light," he remembered, "the mine came in on us."

After the two men had been trapped for some time, Scadding said that they heard shouting and laughter. The survivor insisted that they were all clearheaded and fully conscious.

"At first we thought we must be hearing children playing and we figured there must be a vent to the surface. There wasn't. But we heard it so clearly. Laughing and shouting, like people having fun. It went on for twenty-four hours," Scadding said.

Who could find entertainment value in the plight of miners trapped in a cave-in?

Richard Shaver would quickly nominate his dero for such a dubious distinction. Or was it only a bizarre trick of the mind that made Scadding and the others certain they were hearing the sounds of laughter and merriment?

Shreds of Mysterious Animal Flesh Brought Up in Drill Bits

In the spring of 1966, newspapers in Darwin, Australia, carried the story of mysterious animal flesh, hairs, and hide that had been brought up during a well-drilling operation at a dept of 102 feet.

According to the newsstories, Norman Jensen, an experienced well-driller, had been boring for water 15 miles from Killarney homestead, about 350 miles south of Darwin. Jensen's drill bit had passed through seven layers of limestone, clay, red soil, and sandstone, when at 102 feet, the bit suddenly struck something soft and rapidly dropped to 111 feet. Certain that the bit had bored through to an underground water course, Jensen lowered a pump to make tests.

Instead of fresh water, the pump coughed up a bucketful of flesh, bones, hide, and hairs.

Constable Roy Harvey agreed with Jensen when the driller told him that he had never seen anything like the gory substance from 102 feet. Chickens at Killarney station ate some of the matter without apparent ill effects, and several days later, it was noted that the remaining material had not yet begun to putrefy.

Dr. W. A. Langsford, Northern Territory Director of Health in Darwin, was quoted as saying that preliminary microscopic examination had revealed the material to be hair and tissue. Dr. Langsford stated that samples had been forwarded to the forensic laboratories in Adelaide for more extensive tests, but that there was a possibility that the matter might even be *human*.

IX

The Planet Atlantis

Since primitive humans crawled out of their caves and gazed up in awe at the star-filled night, mankind has been intrigued by the unexplained mysteries of the universe. Early myths and legends tell of mysterious objects roaring across the heavens. Scraps of ancient documents reveal phenomenal, unexplained manifestations in the skies. Virtually every religion relates visitations from angels, demons, devils and gods who descended to the earth in ancient times.

With the publicized arrival of the flying saucer in our atmosphere in 1947, modern man was confronted with what he thought was a new celestial mystery. In their efforts to interpret this phenomenon, a band of scholarly UFOlogists dug through old documents and musty records. They discovered that the UFO phenomenon had appeared periodically throughout history.

Gradually, some UFOlogists developed the conviction that our gods, angels, devils, and demons were nothing more than alien visitors from some celestial world or dimension. Many of these same researchers also claim that legendary Atlantis will never be discovered on Earth; they believe that Atlantis may be a superior civilization on some far planet in a dark corner of the universe.

The "Atlantis in the skies" hypothesis is fascinating, far-out, and admittedly bizarre. Any ancient, unexplained mystery is simply attributed to Atlanteans who supposedly seeded, propagated, and still maintain watch over our planet.

Despite these shortcomings, certain researchers have amassed an incredible stack of evidence to support their beliefs. Old historical accounts, ancient legends, and myths are brought forth and dressed up in new garments and fresh interpretations. Researchers have examined the Bible and other religious works and have discovered passages to support their theory of Atlantean-UFO missionaries swooping down out of the skies to counsel humanity. Others have delved into the enigma of time, space, and matter and have assigned the Atlantean location to a site in another dimension.

The possibility of ancient space visitations was explored by Dr. Carl Sagan at the 1966 convention of the American Astronautical Society. "Our tiny corner of the universe may have been visited thousands of times in the past few billions of years," De. Sagan reported. "At least one of these visits may have occurred in historical times."

Dr. Sagan, a gifted scholar, is both a exobiologist and an astronomer. "The earth may have been visited by various galactic civilizations many times (possibly in the order of 10,000) during geological time," he explained. "It is not out of the question that artifacts of these visits still exist, or even that some kind of base is maintained (possibly automatically) within the solar system to provide continuity for successive expeditions."

Scattering a Cosmic Seed

This hypothesis has led the UFOlogists to theorize that *Homo sapiens* may have been seeded on earth; humanity may have been counseled and directed by UFOnauts from the stars. The Rand Corporation has announced there are *billions* of planets in the universe that have the life-sustaining factors found on Earth.

Despite our many theories, we still do not know how man originated on this planet. The Darwinian theory of evolution remains a fascinating, yet unproved, hypothesis, simply because the elusive "missing link" remains undiscovered. The alleged link between man and his anthropoid cousins may have been provided by visitors from another world.

An imaginative proposal has been advanced by Brinsley Le Poer Trench in his book, *The Sky People* (London: Neville Spearman, Ltd., 1960). Mr. Trench developed the iconoclastic concept that *Homo sapiens* was a celestial experiment that quickly created many unforeseen problems.

The English author declares that the fabled Garden of Eden was possibly located on our neighboring planet, Mars. When the Biblical Jehovah is used in scripture, Mr. Trench theorizes, the name refers basically to a race of beings from space: a Host.

He writes ". . . Jehovah, then, is a name adopted quite recently, as such things go, to designate the People from Somewhere Else in space who deliberately created, by means of their genetic science, a race of hu-man beings peculiarly adapted to perform certain definite and predetermined functions. In addition to their adapting hu-man life-forms to their own ideas they probably also made special adaptations of planet and animal forms."

Space Visitors in Ancient Egypt

Both Mr. Trench and other UFOlogists have pointed to the possibility of ancient space visitors in Egypt. The controversial Tulli papyrus was found among the papers of Professor Alberto Tulli, former director of the Egyptian Museum of the Vatican, Rome. Despite some lost sections, the papyrus was translated by Prince Boris de Rachewiltz, known as one of the world's most expert Egyptologists. The ancient writing was attributed to the Royal Annals of Pharaoh Thutmose III, who lived from 1483 to 1450 B.C.

The translation reads: ". . . In the third month of winter in the year 22, at the sixth hour of the day, the scribes of the House of Life found that there was a circle of fire coming in the sky. (Though) it had no head, the breath from the mouth had a foul odor. One Rod (approximately 150 feet) long was its body and one rod wide, and it had no voice. And the hearts of the scribes became terrified and confused and they laid themselves flat on their bellies ...

". . . Now, after some days had gone by, behold, these things (the fire circles) became more numerous in the skies than ever. They shone more than the brightness of the sun, and extended to the limits of the four supports (or quarters) of the heavens . . . Powerful were the position of these fire circles in the sky . . . It was after supper. Thereupon, these (fire circles) ascended higher in the sky towards the south. (Then) fishes and volatiles fell down from the sky. A marvel never before known since the foundation of this land, Egypt. And the Pharaoh caused incense to be brought to pacify the hearth . . ."

Many people consider the account to be nothing more than the imaginative fantasies of some ancient Egyptian scribes or an elaborate contemporary hoax. Others believe the Tulli fragments may offer an account of an ancient visitation from space beings.

Writing in the May-June, 1966, issue of Britain's *Flying Saucer Review,* Roberto Pinotti discussed the papyrus. "It is safe to say that our picture will never be perfectly clear, since too many details have been altered and facts misrepresented throughout the ages. Nevertheless, if we examine the Tulli papyrus, we can't help wondering if Extraterrestrial creatures visited our planet in the past, and if—as some savants are beginning to suspect—most of our religions and mythologies were really originated by the deification of ancient space visitors who came down among men in far-off times . . ."

The Sons of God

As Pinotti points out, many religions and myths claim that humanity was counseled by divine beings from the heavens. In the Judeo-Christian scriptures, we can find many biblical references to visitors who might have come from other planets. Some UFOlogists claim the "sons of God" mentioned in the Bible were visitors from outer space, possibly a planet known as Atlantis. In *Genesis* (6:4) we find:

". . . And it came to pass, when man began to multiply on the face of the earth, and daughters were born unto them. That the sons of God saw the daughters of men that they were fair; and they took them wives of all which they chose."

Some UFOlogists wonder if these remarks concerning the "daughters of men" mating with the "sons of God" may refer to UFOnauts and our own females. There are many other descriptions of possible space visitors in the Bible. UfO researchers are intrigued by the apocryphal Book of Enoch. The ancient manuscript declares that Noah was an unusual individual, far different in appearance from his brothers, sisters, and playmates.

Was Noah a Star Person?

In an article in the *British Medical Journal*, Professor Arnold Sosby analyzed the legend of Noah. He quoted ancient descriptions of Noah as a person with "a body white as snow, hair white as wool, and eyes that are like the rays of the sun." Professor Sosby informed his colleagues that such a description indicates that Noah may have been an albino.

Professor Sosby's article also referred to passages in the Dead Sea Scrolls, which told of Noah's mother, Bat-Enosh, being suspected of infidelity when the strange young baby was born. In the Book of Enoch, Bat-Enosh tells Lamech, the father, that the child is truly his son.

"He is not the child of any stranger," she insisted, *"nor of the watchers, nor of the sons of heaven."*

The Book of Enoch claimed the "watchers" were two hundred fallen angels. Other apocryphal sources claim they were the "Georgoroi," other visitors from the heavens.

As a long-time student of the Bible and various other sacred writings, Brad Steiger has sought answers to the mystery of the "worlds before Adam was" in holy literature. Here he is in Jerusalem, the Holy city of three of the world's major religions.

The Might of the Fallen Angels

Orthodox religious scripture also lends credence to the theory that astronauts from other worlds may have been visiting Earth during biblical times. The sudden destruction of Sodom and Gomorrah has led Russian Professor M. M. Agrest to suggest that the cities were devastated by an ancient nuclear blast. Moscow's *Literary Gazette* published the professor's theory, which proposed that the ruins of the two cities were fused together under the searing heat of a pre-paleolithic atomic explosion.

In Genesis 19:1-28, we are informed that Lot is waiting by the community gate of Sodom when two angels come walking up to him. The theorists declare that Lot must have made prior arrangements to meet these angels. After their meeting, Lot escorts the angels to his home where they are fed and lodged.

If these angels were wholly spiritual entities, they would certainly not have been interested in an evening dinner, nor in a bed for the night. Neither would they have walked into the town.

Later, when the gay blades of Sodom knocked on Lot's door and demanded to "know" his visitors sexually, the angels must have employed some kind of unusual weapon which instantly blinded the Sodomists and blotted out their lust.

When Lot was informed that Sodom would be destroyed, he still remained in the city. Lot's family considered the warning to be a practical joke. When morning rose, the angels urged Lot and his family to flee.

". . . the men [angels] laid hold upon his hand, and upon the hand of his wife, and upon the hand of his two daughters," we read in Genesis. "The Lord being merciful unto him; and they brought them forth and set him outside the city. And it came to pass when they had brought them forth abroad, that he said, Escape for thy life; look not behind thee, neither stay thou in the plain; escape to the mountains, less thou be consumed . . . haste thee, escape thither; for I cannot do anything till thou come thither."

Believers in the God-Spaceman hypothesis maintain that a nuclear device had been triggered and the "angels" were spiriting Lot and his family away from the blast area. They also point to the passage (Genesis 19:28) where Abraham, Lot's uncle, looks toward the cities of Sodom and Gomorrah in the dawning and sees the smoke of the country going up "as the smoke of a furnace."

Those who subscribe to Professor Agrest's theory feel that the destruction of Sodom and Gomorrah in Genesis offers the perfect description of a nuclear blast. Perhaps alien astronauts had become concerned by the sin and perversion in those cities, some UFOlogists reason, and they utilized an atomic bomb as the fastest way of eliminating the transgressors from the earth.

Atlantis in the Skies

Researchers who combine Atlantean lore and UFOlogy have created several fascinating theories regarding visitations in ancient times by beings from another world.

Some of these theorists ask us to consider the probability that superior, alien beings visited the earth in antediluvian times. These alien hominids may have pointed to the skies and remarked that they came from "Atlantis" — a planet in our own galaxy or some other cluster of stars. These UFOnauts may have described Atlantis as a utopian civilization with superior technology.

Such stories would have been spread by word-of-mouth, through priestly castes and wandering minstrels. Perhaps, to lend additional credence to the tale, narrators may have changed the location of Atlantis to a lost continent on our own planet.

One popular theory has it that Atlantis was a super civilization on earth in some dim epoch of history that was endangered by an impending catastrophe — the advent of an ice age, earthquakes, the gradual shifting of the polar regions, or nuclear war. Whatever the danger, the technologically advanced country attempted to send colonists to another planet, and a few thousand survivors found an Earth-like planet in outer space.

Eventually, there was a longing for the planet of birth. In time, the Atlanteans sent back scout ships to Earth. They discovered that a few humans had survived the Atlantean disaster, but they were living as primitive cavemen with no knowledge of the grandeur that had been Atlantis. The returning astronauts counseled humanity in the arts of agriculture, law, religion, and social structure, and told their struggling cousins wondrous tales of the lost Atlantis.

Under this hypothesis, our modern world is a product of Atlantean knowledge and technology.

The sacred Hindu hymns, the *Rig-Veda*, constitute some of the oldest known religious documents. The splendid poetry tells of the achievements of the Hindu gods, and one passage tells of Indra, a god-being, who was honored when his name was turned into "India."

Indra, who became known as the "fort destroyer" because of his exploits in war, was said to travel through the skies in a flying machine, the Vimana. This craft was allegedly equipped with awesome weapons capable of destroying a city. Their effect seems to have been like that of a laser beam, or a nuclear device. Another ancient Indian text, the *Mahabharata*, tells of an attack on an enemy army:

> . . . It was as if the elements had been unfurled. The sun spun around in the heavens. The world shuddered in fever, scorched by the terrible heat of this weapon. Elephants burns into flames . . . The rivers boiled. Animals crumpled to the ground and died. The armies of the enemy were mowed down when the raging of the elements reached them. Forests collapsed in splintered rows. Horses and chariots were burned up . . . The corpses of the fallen were mutilated by the terrible heat so that they looked other than human . . . Never before had we heard of such a ghastly weapon.

The Sky People

Dare we believe that the legends and myths of our ancestors are based on fact? If so, we may discover that humanity's history is in dire need of revision. Ancient manuscripts are crammed with numerous accounts of sky discs, flying chariots, cloud ships, and aerial demons.

An example of such visits allegedly occurred in A.D. 840 when farmers, peasants, and tradesmen in Europe were forbidden to barter with the "sky people." The Archbishop of Lyons, Argobard, was visibly upset because his parishioners believed in "ships from the clouds." The aerial ships were supposedly piloted by beings of normal, human-like appearance from the "land beyond the clouds — Magonia."

The occupants of the ships were certainly not supernatural beings. They traded artifacts and coins to French peasants for earthly fruit and vegetables.

In *Contra Insulem Vivgi Opinionem*, Archbishop Argobard reported on the capture of a crew from one of the Magonian flying machines.

"A certain assembly exhibited several people as captives," he wrote. "Three men and one woman, as if they had fallen from the ship themselves. They had been detained for some days in chains, then finally put on show to the mob, and as I have said, in our presence they were stoned to death. . . ."

Such incidents undoubtedly led the "sky people" to establish elaborate security measures when they next landed on Earth.

Throughout the dim corridors of history, we can find frequent mention of the legendary "sky people." Often these beings are considered to have been emissaries of the "flying serpent." The snake-worshipping Aztecs and Mayans are not far removed from the Chinese cultists, who worshipped a celestial dragon. Both races may have been contacted by emissaries from a cosmic Atlantis.

The Enigma of Sumer

According to the historians, one afternoon 7,000 years ago, our ancestors suddenly decided to establish the Sumerian civilization. Until then, man had clubbed and fought his way through a primitive world. Overnight, the nomads and hunters created a miraculous city-state in the Mesopotamian valley—the beginning of our present civilization.

With little effort, these primitive tribesmen left their tents and caves and became skilled in the arts of civilized living. They constructed homes, temples, towers, churches, and pyramids. They left the risky rewards of hunting and became farmers, tending the soil and irrigating the land. They became experts in metals, ceramics, and hundreds of other skills.

The Sumerians created a cuneiform writing. They built observatories for their astronomers and studied the stars. Their astronomers were so accurate that their measurements on the rotation of the moon is off only -.3 from modern, computerized figures. At the height of the Greek civilization, the highest known number was 10,000. After that sum, the Greeks could only fall back on "infinity." The Sumerians were master mathematicians, and a tablet found on the Kunyunjik hills a few years ago contained a 15-digit number— 195,955,200,000,000.

The Sumerian astronomers charted the stars as accurately as our modern scientists. One pictograph depicts the planets revolving around the sun—something that Copernicus and Kepler postulated only 500 years ago. Sumerian drawings show human-like beings with helmets of stars. Other figures are drawn zooming through the skies on celestial, starred discs, or spheres.

Historians have a habit of dismissing legends about the origin of civilizations and nations, and they have discarded the Sumerians' own account of how their remarkable city-state was established.

When Dr. Carl Sagan collaborated with Dr. Joseph S. Shklovski, the noted Russian scientist, on *Intelligent Life in the Universe*, he discussed the ancient Sumerian tablets known as *Ancient Fragments*, possibly a first-hand account of how civilization started:

". . . Ancient writers present an account of a remarkable series of events. Sumerian civilization is depicted by the descendent of the Sumerians themselves to be of non-human origin. A succession of strange creatures appears over a course of several generations. Their only apparent purpose is to instruct mankind. Oannes and other Apkallu (strange creatures) are described variously as 'animals endowed with reason,' as 'beings,' as 'semi-demons,' and as 'personages.' They are never described as gods."

A Babylonian priest and historian, Berosus, declared that the Sumerians once "lived like beasts in the field with no order or rule." The Sumerians lived exactly like their primitive forefathers until the bizarre "beast with reason" appeared in their midst.

The gifted entity was endowed with a superior intelligence, but its appearance was frightening to behold. An amphibian, the "Oannes," had the body of a fish, human-like feet on the end of the fish tail, and both a fish head and a human head.

Berosus explained that this fantastic fish-man walked about on land, counseled the ancient Sumerians, but returned to the ocean each evening.

". . . This being in daytime used to converse with men," Berosus wrote. "But, it took no food at that season; and he gave them insight into letters and sciences and every kind of art. He taught them to construct houses, to found temples, to compile laws, and explained to them the principles of geometrical knowledge. He made them distinguish the seeds of the earth, and showed them how to collect fruits. In short, he instructed them in everything which could tend to soften the manners and humanize mankind."

Let us assume that you are an alien hominid from the Planet Atlantis sent to Earth to instruct the primitive inhabitants on the rudiments of civilization. Let us also presume that *Homo sapiens* was seeded there many generations ago; it is now time to pass along knowledge from the mother planet. You will need a safe, secure headquarters or your crewmen and the spaceship, which is capable of underwater propulsion. Wouldn't you submerge your craft in a quiet lagoon and emerge on land each morning in an underwater scuba diving suit? If we allow our imagination to expand, we can see ancient scribes attempting to describe a conventional diving suit, "both a fish head and a human head."

Brinsley le Poer Trench has declared his belief in the factual elements of mythology. "It is shorthand," he said. "Mythology is condensed history."

Amerindian Legends of Metallic Eagles

Legends of the Eskimos of the far north tell of how their ancestors were flown to the polar region by god-like beings with metallic wings.

Farther south, we discover a Mayan tale of a gigantic metallic eagle landing from the heavens with "the roar of a lion." The "beak" of the "eagle" opened and ". . . four creatures strange to our tribe, who did not breathe the air we breathe, walked from the marvelous eagle."

The mythology of Peru says that the inhabitants of that area were born on earth from silver, bronze, and golden eggs "which floated down from the heavens."

The *Popul Vuh*, which is the bible of the Quiches tribe of Guatemala, outlines another Mayan legend concerning visitors from the skies. These unusual beings possessed and used the compass. They knew the world was round.

The *Popul Vuh* also related that these sky people knew the secrets of the universe, and when the tribesmen became determined to steal these secrets, the visitors fogged the earthmen's minds.

Were these unusual sky people the survivors of the Atlantean disaster? Were they from a planet named Atlantis? Or, as we have discussed in a previous chapter, is Atlantis a hidden, highly developed undersea base for alien visitors to our world?

Homo sapiens views the universe through a slender speck of the visual spectrum, between 254 millimicrons on the one side to 2,400 millimicrons on the other. We are looking out of our own world through a tiny crack and, perhaps arrogantly, proclaiming the dimensions of being.

History is equally limited in its view of the past; few records exist of prior civilizations. Man's past is hidden in a mist of secrets, misunderstandings, and contradictions.

There are many mysteries about Atlantis, the fabled land. There are few definite answers.

X

Does The Rising Of Atlantis Herald Armageddon?

O n August 23, 1968, a Canadian broadcast journalist excitedly
tore the following news item from the studio Teletype and put
it in an envelope addressed to me:

ATLANTIS

MIAMI, FLORIDA — A NOTED ARCHEOLOGIST REPORTS WHAT HE CALLS
"EXCITING AND DISTURBING" DISCOVERY IN BAHAMIAN WATERS OF AN
ANCIENT "TEMPLE." DOCTOR MANSON VALENTINE SPECULATES IT MIGHT BE
PART OF THE LEGENDARY LOST CONTINENT OF ATLANTIS.

DOCTOR VALENTINE SAYS THE MYSTERIOUS FIND IN SIX FEET OF WATER
OFF A BAHAMIAN ISLAND IS "THE FIRST OF ITS KIND IN THE WESTERN
HEMISPHERE." THE ARCHEOLOGIST IS A ONE-TIME ZOOLOGY PROFESSOR AT
YALE UNIVERSITY.

AFTER INSPECTING THE FIND LAST WEEKEND, DOCTOR VALENTINE SAID
THE TOP IS ABOUT TWO FEET ABOVE THE OCEAN FLOOR. HE ADDED: "THE
WALLS ARE SLOPING. I DUG INTO THE SAND AND MANAGED TO FEEL ABOUT
ANOTHER THREE FEET DOWN. IT IS OBVIOUSLY MUCH DEEPER, BUT WE WILL
NOT KNOW HOW MUCH UNTIL WE EXCAVATE. THE MATERIAL IS A KIND OF
MASONRY AND IT IS DEFINITELY MAN-MADE."

Earlier that summer, Robert Brush, a pilot, who had been flying between Miami and Nassau, spotted a square structure in shallow water off the northern tip of Andros Island in the Bahamas. Brush told Dr. Valentine of his sighting and also passed the information along to noted underwater explorer Dmitri Rebikoff, who, while airborne in 1967, had noticed what he had assessed as a man-made rectangular construction under the surface of the Grand Bahama Bank.

Valentine and Rebikoff launched a preliminary expedition to the site at once and found that the structure measured 60 by 100 feet, with walls three feet thick. The limestone blocks which formed the walls had been placed with a skill in masonry that lay beyond the talents of recent inhabitants of the area.

Atlantis Rises in Bimini

Edgar Cayce enthusiasts were ecstatic at the press releases of an Atlantean temple "rising" in the Great Bahama Bank. One of the sleeping prophet's more startling predictions had been that in 1968 and 1969 remains of Atlantis would begin to rise from the sea near the Bimini Islands, and now it seemed that the clairvoyant's prognostication had hit the location exactly.

According to his entranced reading, in August of 1926 Cayce had first named the Bimini Islands as providing the most accessible remains of the Atlantean civilization. He was giving a reading for a group of men in search of oil and buried treasure in those same islands: ". . . this is the highest portion left above the waves of a once great continent, upon which the civilization as now exists in the world's history found much of that as would be used as means for attaining that civilization. . . ." (996-1)

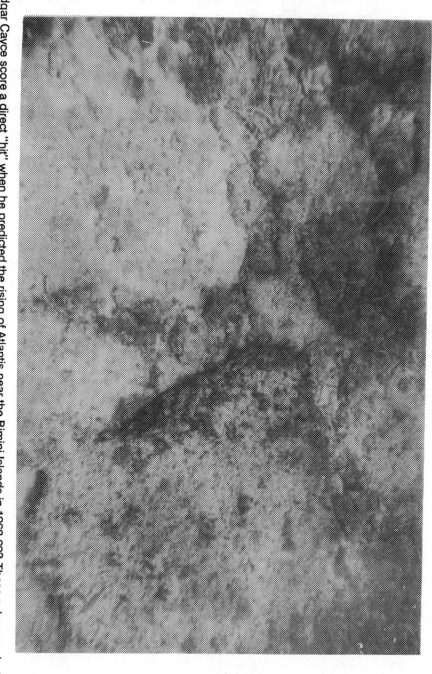

Did Edgar Cayce score a direct "hit" when he predicted the rising of Atlantis near the Bimini Islands in 1968-69? These submerged ruins of ancient cities were discovered in the area at that time.

In March of 1927, Cayce answered the question whether the continent he saw on Bimini was that of Alta or Poseidia (Atlantis) by saying: "A temple of the Poseidians was in a portion of this land."

According to the files of the Association for Research and Enlightenment at Virginia Beach, Virginia, the next reference to Atlantean artifacts in the area of Bimini was produced in a series of thirteen rather lengthy readings on Atlantis given in 1932, which ended with the words: "The British West Indies or the Bahamas, and a portion of the same that may be seen in the present — if the geological survey would be made in some of these — especially, or notably, in Bimini and in the Gulf Stream through this vicinity, these may be even yet determined." (364-3)

Dr. Valentine does believe in the existence of Atlantis, but not because of what Edgar Cayce or any other mystic may have seen in a vision. He regrets that the popular press enthusiastically seized upon news of the discovery of the structure at Bimini and transformed it into an Atlantean temple.

After further investigation, he feels that the site may have been constructed by the Mayans or some other pre-Colombian native culture. It has been pointed out that, by strange coincidence, the site duplicates the floor plan of the Mayan "Temple of the Turtles" at Uxmal in Yucatan.

Dr. Valentine believes in Atlantis because he considers one of the great mysteries of the deep past to be the apparent suddenness with which highly evolved culture patterns throughout the prehistoric world have disappeared (in Peru, in the Pacific, in Cambodia, in Lebanon and elsewhere), leaving not a trace of the fate of their creators.

"Might not these unaccountable demises have been the aftermath of violent earth spasms of which there appear to have been at least four during and terminating the geological epoch known as the Pleistocene?" Dr. Valentine wonders.

"There is good reason to believe that only eleven or twelve thousand years have elapsed since the last of these titanic upheavals shook the earth. Unfortunately, man's early history has not only been physically obscured by such drastic, world-wide explosions of nature, but has been subjectively clouded by the persistent, yet erroneous, theory that, until recent times, man had never evolved beyond a state of primitive savagery."

Dr. Valentine joins other bold thinking scientists in bemoaning the fact that the anthropological and biological disciplines, "despite overwhelming evidence to the contrary, are still reluctant to relinquish the century-old theories of Darwin and Lyell who flatly contended that only slow, gradual changes in evolution and geology were possible." Without long stretches of uneventful time, Darwin's theory of evolution by natural selection would lose plausibility.

"Thus was born the school of 'Uniformitarianism' in direct contrast to the more objective views of those earth scientists who have come to recognize the principles of periodic stress build-up in the planet's magnetic field, with consequent, swift environmental changes at the breaking point. The concept of a subcontinental island in mid Atlantic ('Atlantis'), lost through catastrophic assault, is by no means alien to the latter philosophy," Dr. Valentine states.

In his prospectus for an expedition in search of a "Precataclysmic Civilization and Evidence for the Sunken Continent of 'Atlantis,' " Dr. Valentine argues that there can now be no reasonable doubt that a "highly evolved, precataclysmic civilization did exist." In Dr. Valentine's view, the 'dawn ' people were far from primitives, but expressed their religious cults and advanced metaphysical knowledge in a universal system, "a fact which in itself suggests an uncomprehended ability to travel widely."

An Interview with Dr. J. Manson Valentine

The extremely busy but always gracious Dr. Manson Valentine granted me an interview regarding his much-publicized find and his plans for future expeditions:

I have a copy of the teletype from August 23, 1968, in which you announce your "exciting and disturbing discovery of an ancient temple."

DR. J. MANSON VALENTINE: It could be a sacred site, but that was certainly not a temple, as far as we know. I had been surveying from the air and doing a little diving in the whole area of the Bimini chain, and I had found what I considered to be a valid indication of human habitation and designed artifactual patterns on the windward and the leeward sides of all the keys all the way down to Orange Key.

You said that the structure duplicated the floor plan of the Mayan "Temple of the Turtles" at Uxmal in Yucatan.

Yes, it is exactly the same shape, same dimensions — 100 feet by 60 — and the east side if partitioned off, just as it is in the Temple of the Turtles. And the corners of the west side, particularly the southwest corner, is also partitioned off just as it is in the Yucatan temple.

Have you found any artifacts other than the edifices?

Not yet. But we have some very amazing sites that look like cities over an extensive area of the ocean bottom. We have subsequently discovered a very important site east of Bimini. There is a sort of dike there, a great dam of twenty-foot long blocks, concentric circles, and areas where the blocks are marked. It actually looks like an ancient dam that could have impounded fresh water in a reservoir — and the relics of that reservoir still appear in the form of a great rectangle.

We have discovered at least fifty sites. One time coming up from Bogatá, from six miles up, we noticed tremendous artifacts. We have yet to rediscover them, but they are there. At one place there is a definite arrow-shaped construction that points to the northwest. We have also found a domicile that is white in contrast to the dark bottom.

Atlantis and the New Age

If I may be permitted to make one last metaphysical speculation of my own, let us consider, for the purpose of discussion, that the structure sighted beneath the ocean off Bimini is precisely what many of these individuals with a somewhat mystical bent are certain that it is—the remnants of an Atlantean temple. Let us suppose that Edgar Cayce has scored a bull's eye and has accurately predicted the "rising" of Atlantis, beginning with the discovery of the remains in 1968. Now, still maintaining our mystical approach to the subject, we must answer the question why a bit of Atlantis should bob to the surface at that particular moment in history.

We often hear the proclamation that we stand at the dawning of the Age of Aquarius, a new age of harmony, peace, love, and understanding. Might it be that before each new age is allowed to dawn, the preceding age must be set into obscurity?

We are now suggesting a reason why a cataclysm may have destroyed the antediluvian Atlantis so completely, and it is a reason that the pragmatically orthodox may find scientifically offensive and the mystical seekers may find spiritually uncomfortable. That bit of temple that worked its way to the surface off Bimini, you see, may be a portent heralding the sunset of our own epoch, our Armageddon.

According to tradition, Armageddon, the final battle between the sons of God and the minions of Satan, will be waged in the Garden of Eden, where the human race originated and began its rebellion against God. Human history will, consequently, come to an end where it began.

If the souls of men first entered flesh on Atlantis, as Edgar Cayce has envisioned, rather than somewhere in the Euphrates Valley, and if human corruption and spiritual rebellion were first encountered on that Atlantic kingdom, then the battleground may be re-emerging for that ultimate clash of Good versus Evil in our epoch.

The Remarkable Frescoes
in the Dechany Monastery

The notion that the "Elect" (or those of the proper vibratory level) will be carried off in "chariots of the Lord" is by no means a recent addition to orthodox religious teaching. We may only speculate about what traditions may have been lost to us when such discoveries are made as those in the Dechany Monastery in Kosovskaya Metchia, southern Yugoslavia.

Built in the first half of the fourteenth century, the Dechany Monastery contains numerous frescoes of scenes from the Old and New Testaments. According to Vyacheslav Zaitesev, writing in *Sputnik*, [the Russian equivalent of *Reader's Digest*], one fresco depicts two "chariots" flying west to east. The being in either ship has no halo or any of the traditional accouterments of angels.

The Yugoslav magazine *Svet* writes: "Both ships have streamlined bodies. Clearly visible jets in their wake accentuate the impression of speed. The saints in the flying machines are in the positions of pilots. Angels watching the flight cover their eyes and ears with their hands and seem to be backing away for fear of being blinded or deafened. . . ."

Zaitesev says that the fresco depicting the Resurrection of Christ appears just as strangely space-aged as the others. "The messiah looks as he is in a rocket which has not yet begun to move. Indeed, the vehicle looks very much like a space rocket, with a two-wing stabilizer in its upper part. With his right hand Christ is trying to lift aboard the ship one of the people standing on the ground before starting on his way to the heavenly kingdom."

Investigators from Yugoslavia who quizzed the monks at Dechany about their unusual frescoes were told that the drawings of the "spaceships" were pictures of the sun and the moon. According to New Testament legend, the monks told their visitors, Christ was crucified during a solar eclipse. Why the sun was depicted as rising in the west, though, the monks could not clarify.

Svet says that an ancient paper in the monastery refers to a legend declaring that Christ was a man who came down to Earth from space. The Yugoslav periodical comments that such ideas may be "overbold," but the strange frescoes, depicting objects resembling space capsules, baffle scientist and specialist as well as layman.

"The Dechany frescoes are not unique," Vyacheslav Zaitesev goes on. "An icon in the Church Archaeology Study in the Moscow

Theological Academy, called 'The Resurrection of Jesus Christ' and dating back to the 17th century, shows Christ in a streamlined container which vaguely resembles a spaceship standing on the ground. Smoke billows from both sides of the container's lower part, enveloping the legs of the angels who watch from the sidelines. Just as on the Dechany fresco, Christ's right hand lifts a man (the church identifies him as Adam). Eve waits her turn on the other side."

The Fifth World of the Hopis

According to Frank Waters and Oswald White Bear Fredericks, who assembled the *Book of the Hopi*, the Hopi Indians also predicted that we stand on the threshold of both an Armageddon and the start of a new cycle in the Fifth World. The United States will be destroyed in a war started by the "old countries" that first received the light (i.e. India, China, Egypt, Palestine, Africa). Only the homeland of the Hopis will serve as an oasis to which refugees from radioactivity might flee.

The last great war, the Hopis tell us, will be ". . . a spiritual conflict with material matters. Material matters will be destroyed by spiritual beings who will remain to create one world and one nation under one power, that of the Creator."

The Armageddon of spiritual against material will occur when the "Saquasohuh (Blue Star) Kachina" — now represented by a far away and yet invisible blue star — makes its appearance. The Emergence into the Fifth World, however, has already begun, the Hopis state.

Amerindian Legends of Terrible Floods

Each of the Amerindian tribes with which I am familiar cherishes legends that tell of their people emerging from the destruction that had been visited upon a former civilization. The majority of the accounts deal with the surviving peoples having escaped from a terrible flood, which immediately suggests both the biblical story of The Deluge and the Atlantis mythos.

The Yuchi Indians, who lived in what is now South Carolina and Georgia tell of a big flood that drowned all but those who had been warned of the impending disaster. After the flood, goes the legend, the survivors attempted to build a high tower in which to take refuge should such a deluge again strike Earth. But such an enterprise brought only a differing of speech among the workers and a subsequent scattering of the people. (The latter account is highly reminiscent of the biblical Tower of Babel.)

The Arkansas Indians told of a destructive flood that was sent to Earth from God because of man's great wickedness. The more pious survivors made their way to the North American continent in order to remain separate from others who might again become corrupt.

The Navajos say that their ancestors escaped the terrible flood through a long, hollow reed. When they reached safety, they were taken in spirit through space to visit other worlds, the Moon, the stars. After the waters had subsided on Earth, they returned to live on the mountains and in the cliffs. The world will again be destroyed if man cannot control his wickedness.

The Mandan Indians believed their ancestors rode out the flood in a big canoe, which came to rest on a mountain when the waters subsided.

The Delaware, or the Lenni-Lenapi, recounted the story of a continuing struggle between the men of Earth and the Snake-People. Resolving to destroy mankind, the Snake-People brought about a great rushing of waters to drown all men. A female spirit helped some men to a boat and saw them to safety. The immigrants landed first in a cold country, but gradually worked their way to a more temperate land. In the meantime, the Snake-People migrated to the east and conquered a prosperous nation. Some of the Delaware remained in the new land, while others made their way back home.

The Popul Vuh, sacred book of the Central American Indians, states the flood myth in this way:

"Then the waters were agitated by the will of the Heart of Heaven, and a great inundation came . . . upon heads of these creatures. . . . They were engulfed, and a resinous thickness descended from heaven . . . the face of the Earth was obscured, and a heavy darkening rain commenced — rain by day and rain by night. There was heard a great noise above their heads, as if produced by fire. Then were men seen running, pushing each other, filled with despair. They wished to climb upon the trees, and the trees shook them off. They wished to enter into the caves, and the caves closed before them. Water and fire contributed to the universal ruin at the time of the last great cataclysm, which preceded the fourth creation."

The principal point of each of the Amerindian myths of destruction and rebirth is that civilization is cyclical, continually being born, struggling toward a Golden Age, then slipping backward into moral morass, forward into its death throes . . . only to be reborn so that the process may begin once more.

The Seven Worlds of the Seneca

The Seven Worlds legend has been revealed to few outside of those who are a part of the oral tradition of the Seneca. In my book *Medicine Talk* I included the legend in its entirety, which was translated by Twylah Nitsch, Repositor of Seneca Wisdom. For our purposes here, I will quote portions of sections after *Swen-i-o* (the Great Mystery) has created the heavens, Earth, and all creatures upon our terrestrial ball:

The First World

The nations of the First World emerged at the place where the Sun raised its head above the rim of the sky. At this place Mother Earth shared her gifts in great profusion. But the people at that time were not grateful for these gifts and caused a disease of waste to visit Nature Land.

Swen-i-o [The Great Mystery or Spirit] looked at man and arranged a time for the first decree: "You are creatures of nature, created by me to live always in true harmony. Wisdom, if learned, is balanced of life. Breaking this lay, breeds misery and strife."

For a time, the people were impressed by the Great Revelation they had heard, but they soon found it very hard to follow the decree of the Great Spirit.

As time passed, the decree was forgotten, and *Swen-i-o* arranged for a cleansing of the First World.

He placed a blanket of protection over those creatures who honored his decree. He ordered the Sun to use its power in cleansing the First World. The power of the Sun caused the devastation of the First World.

The Dawn of the Second World

The lessons learned from the acts of the people who perished in the First World remained in the minds of those who were saved. Carefully they populated the Second World. Their culture was superb, and it spread rapidly throughout the Second World.

Migrations moved toward the North, a place of total whiteness; to the South, a place of total darkness; with the nations adapting to the environment of these places. Their outer skin became faded where it was cold, and dark where it was hot. Migrations followed the Sun as he travelled the path of the Sky Dome from East to West.

Before long, it became evident that the people of the Second World were following in the footsteps of their predecessors, who had inhabited the First World. Those who still honored the decree of the Great Spirit were given a blanket of protection, and the cleansing of the Second World was begun.

Swen-i-o ordered the Sun to withdraw its warmth from the face of Mother Earth, leaving only the Moon to exert his power upon Nature Land. The lesser light of the Moon was unable to warm

Mother Earth. A state of cold settled upon Nature Land. This caused the devastation of the Second World.

The Third World

The Third World was inhabited by people and creatures with gifts and abilities that surpassed the two previous worlds. They spread their influence along the path of the Sun, establishing magnificent civilizations and cultures, populating more than half of the world. Four races had evolved as a result of migrations; the white, the red, the yellow, and the black — their complexions and physical characteristics having adapted to the environment in which they lived.

During the Third World the four races became more aware of the laws that governed Nature Land, and they made some effort to learn about its mystery. For this reason their civilization flourished for a longer period than the first and second worlds. But in spite of their knowledge, they became forgetful, and they consistently brought disruption upon the gifts of Mother Earth.

For the third time, those who honored the decree of *Swen-i-o* were placed under the blanket of protection. Water, the third creation of *Swen-i-o*, was responsible for the cleansing of the Third World.

In the Mind of *Swen-i-o* came the Dawn of the Fourth World

The migrations of the Fourth World completed the population of the universe from East to West. The greatest span of existence was experienced by the people evolving in the Fourth World, because this world was the Middle World. Those whose evolvement had reached the awakening period were willing to share their knowledge with others. They began to keep records; but the greatest records were still in the minds of the generations who had lived under the Blanket of Protection and who still honored the decree of the Great Spirit. These people had evolved along the thread that connected them to *Swen-i-o*, the creator.

During the Fourth World, the inhabitants became aware of the universal stream that revolved around the world, and they learned the wisdom of enlightenment. Through the minds of these people the Secret of the Ages was recorded.

Unfortunately, too many still pursued the materialistic path, spreading misery and doom among the inhabitants.

The cleansing of the Fourth World was exerted by the combined efforts of the Sun, the Moon, and Water upon Mother Earth. The Fourth World's corruption had been the greatest — therefore, its need for renewal, the greatest.

In The Mind of *Swen-i-o* was the Dawn of the Fifth World

The greatest strides in understanding took place in the Fifth World. The era of the awakening had become established, and man found self-satisfaction in sharing his gifts and abilities with others. The Records of the Ages were being uncovered, and the false documents of man were being corrected.

The duration of the Fifth World was short compared to the previous worlds. His lessons were extremely difficult, but he had achieved self-mastery. However, he had not yet convinced the duality of his nature regarding the function of his spiritual mind over the physical body. Wars within his attitudes and thoughts still festered in his mind, creating injustices upon the gifts of Mother Earth.

Repeatedly, there had been messengers of the Great Spirit to remind the people of the wisdom of harmony. Yet they were unable to perpetuate their beliefs after the general disturbances of their way of life in the latter days of the Fourth World.

Mother Earth was again in need of a renewal of her gifts. The cleansing was exerted by the powers of the Sun and Moon and was completed in the mind of *Swen-i-o* the Creator.

The Dawn of the Sixth World

The Sixth World had the shortest evolvement period. It was the world that opened the eyes of man. . . . He . . . recognized the necessity of fitting into a pattern that functioned in unison with his world. As yet, he had not fully accepted the laws of nature as his guide. His life at times was still governed by his own selfish thinking. There had to be one more cleansing to renew the gifts of Mother Earth before man truly understood and could practice his purpose in life.

For all six worlds, man had wreaked havoc upon
    himself, his fellow man, and the creatures
    of Nature.
Now he stood at the threshold of perfection,
    awaiting the wisdom of the ages to
    penetrate his mind.

The cleansing of the Sixth World was exerted by the power of the Moon, followed by the heating properties of the Water, which paved the way for the dawn of the Seventh World.

The Seventh World

In the Seventh World, the Happy Hunting Ground, Man saw beauty everywhere.
He listened to the music of the Universe.
And sang his part in the chorus.
He felt love for *Swen-i-o* and for his fellow-man.
He shared his gifts and abilities with others.
He made the Seventh World a place of peace and happiness.

The final cleansing had been completed, and man's life was guided by a spiritual light, the same light that is in the mind of *Swen-i-o*, the Great Spirit.

The Seneca Legend of the Seven Worlds says that the world of man has relived the traumatic experiences of birth, death, and rebirth six times before and that we stand on the brink of destruction prior to entering the final world in our evolutionary cycle.

For the Amerindian traditionalist, the destructions of the previous worlds have been a necessary part of humankind's spiritual evolution. Man forgets the lessons of the Great Spirit and falls away to rely upon his own feeble devices. When this state of affairs comes to pass, the Great Spirit causes a time of Great Purification, which cleanses the Earth Mother for a new epoch, a new world.

It is obvious that the Amerindian view of the "worlds before our own" is one of catastrophism, that there have been a succession of cultures created, leveled, then recreated.

It is really too simplistic to state that all those scientists who embrace tenets of the catastrophist school believe that the world is only 6,004 years old and that all uniformitarian geologists believe our planet to be four-and-one-half billion years old. In the February, 1975 issue of *Natural History*, Stephen Jay Gould argues that modern geology is really a blend of concepts from both the uniformitarians and the catastrophists.

In his article, "Catastrophes and Steady State Earth,", Gould writes:

"A 6,000-year-old earth does require a belief in catastrophes to compress the geologic record into so short a time. But the converse is decidedly not true; a belief in catastrophes does not dictate a 6,000-year-old earth. The earth may be 4.5 or, for that matter, 100 billion years old and still build its mountains with great rapidity."

Gould admits: "The geologic record does seem to record catastrophes: rocks are fractured and contorted, whole faunas are wiped out . . . . "

The classic uniformitarian position, as developed by Charles Lyell in 1830 in the first volume of his revolutionary *Principles of Geology*, are summarized by Gould in the following manner:

1.   Natural laws are constant (uniform in space and time). . . This is not a statement about the world; it is an *a priori* claim of method that scientists must make in order to proceed with any analysis of the past. . . .

2.   Processes now operating to mold the earth's surface should be invoked to explain the events of the past (uniformity of process through time). . . . This again is not an argument about the world; it is a statement about scientific procedure. . . .

3.   Geologic change is slow, dual, and steady, not cataclysmic or paroxysmal. . . .

4.   The earth has been fundamentally the same since its formation (uniformity of material conditions). . . .

Lyell's vision of a uniformitarian Earth caused him to reconcile the appearance of direction with dynamic constancy in the history of life by proposing that the entire fossil record represents but one part of a "great year" — a grand cycle that will occur again when ". . . the huge iguanodon might reappear in the woods, and the ichthyosaur in the sea, while the pterodactyle might flit again through umbrageous groves of tree ferns."

The catastrophists pursued the literal view. "They saw direction in the history of life, and they believed it, " Gould remarks. "In retrospect, they were right.

"Modern geology is really an even mixture of two scientific schools — Lyell's original, rigid uniformitarianism and the scientific catastrophism of Cuvier and Agassiz. We accept Lyell's first two uniformities, but so did the catastrophists. Lyell's third uniformity appropriately derigidifies in his great substantive contribution; his fourth (and most important) uniformity has been graciously forgotten. . . ."

Re-examining the Seven Worlds

Re-examining the Seneca legend of the Seven Worlds from a catastrophist's point of view, we find that the First World was destroyed by "the power of the Sun," fire, perhaps, or, might we say, radioactivity?

The Second World, with only the Moon to warm the Earth, may be referring to a great Ice Age, either the one with which we assume familiarity or one in times long before our accepted geologic records.

The destruction of the Third World was brought about by water, perhaps caused by great shifts in the Earth's crust.

The Fourth World is said to have been one of great intellectual accomplishment. There were great migrations, a period of enlightenment and awakening, technological accomplishment. The very Secret of the Ages was recorded.

Could this have been the "world before our own" that bequeathed many of the legendary wonders of the ancient world that appear so out of context with our evaluations of the early states of our epoch? The statement that the Fourth World was destroyed by the combined efforts of Sun, Moon, and Water — fire, ice, flood — could suggest the horrible devastation of nuclear power to the point where some nations were totally destroyed and even submerged.

The Fifth World may have been but a prolongation of the Fourth. Seneca legend records that although awakening of the spirit was evident and many false documents were corrected, the duration of the Fifth World was brief.

We may, in the Fourth World, be remembering a global war of terrible nuclear conflict. An uneasy peace is reached by the survivors, and men of good will on both sides attempt to establish a time of harmony and resurrection. But the sparks of enmity still smolder, and they are ignited by war hawks in a final paroxysm of destruction.

The Sixth World may have been the antediluvian world to which the Old Testament refers, a world once again destroyed by flood.

Or, according to some interpretations, it may be the world in which we are presently striving; for it does not seem as though we have yet attained the Seventh World wherein man "sees beauty everywhere," is attuned to "the music of the Universe," or feels love for God and our fellow man. And if the "power of the Moon" refers to a time of destruction of cold, many authorities have stated their

conviction that we are entering a cold-dry cycle of history prepara-
tory to another Ice Age.

In the holy books and legends of many ancient peoples we find
innumerable accounts of wars between the heavens and the earth.
Cosmic revolutions and civil warms were said to rent and to split the
prehistoric worlds on several occasions. More than one Sodom and
Gomorrah exploded so that "the smoke rose up like that from a
mighty furnace," and references to their destruction are found in the
scriptures of Hindu and Hebrew and in the myths of people as
diverse as the American Indian and the African.

Each of the legends has the extant civilization being decimated.
Its governments are rendered impotent, its commerce abandoned, its
cultural attributes forgotten, its cities crumbled to rubble. But always
a remnant of its people survive. Enough human seed is retained to
perpetuate the stubborn and striving species. The cycle of the death
and rebirth of civilization is maintained. Man returns to the primitive
to relearn the basics, to recall the essentials. At the same time he is
once again mastering the elementary lessons of survival, he is re-
establishing an understanding of his physical body's niche in the web
of life and his ethereal psyche's position in the oneness of the holy,
the divine, the cosmic. It is as if man must continue to replicate the
progression of hunter to farmer to merchant to scientist-philosopher
until he sets it right and graduates from ape to angel.